Creole

Babette de Rozières

Creole

Photographs by Akiko Ida & Pierre Javelle

Contents

I put down my roots in Guadeloupe, where nature is generous and instills a taste for work and play. In the West Indies, the art of cooking comes to us as an inheritance. There is no particular hour for eating. There is always something to taste within arm's reach - a piece of fruit, a fritter, cane juice, coconut sherbet, confectionery such as the delicious kilibibi... West Indians are gourmands by nature.

I am both Guadeloupean and a head chef. My grandmother initiated me into the subtleties of Creole cooking and it was through a sin that I discovered its authentic tastes - yes, I admit it, as soon as she turned her back, I dipped my finger into her sauces, out of pure greed.

Today I cook just as my grandmother taught me. I use fish and shellfish from the Caribbean Sea - mahi mahi, swordfish, snapper, shark, octopus, conch. A great diversity of herbs goes into developing my sauces - scallions, thyme, flat-leaf parsley, bois d'Inde* … and spices also play an important part in any Creole feast, from the celebrated West Indian Colombo powder (curry powder) to graines à roussir, a blend of cumin, fenugreek and mustard seeds. Indeed, the whole secret of Creole cooking is to be found in its spices, and in the way the ingredients are marinaded before cooking, lending our food its incomparable bouquet of aromas.

Led by the winds of history and adventure, Creole cuisine is the happy result of cross-fertilization. It reflects the same diversity of civilizations that characterize the West Indian people themselves, who have come to our islands from Asia, Africa, Europe and the East Indies. Our cuisine is solid and well constructed, however, it remains refined and light and its palette extends well beyond the traditional sweet and sour. Its flavors are not aggressive, partly because the chile we eat is often served separately and added to a dish according to each person's taste. Finally, it is healthy and nutritionally well balanced.

The names and terms specific to the cooking and products of the West Indies are followed by an asterisk and are included in the glossary on page 354.

When enjoying Creole cuisine, your sense of smell functions at full speed and your tastebuds are constantly stimulated. Its tastes can surprise but they can never disappoint. It awakens the senses and never leaves you indifferent. Its aromas are seductive, as is its hint of pungency. You succumb to its charms at once and will never forget them.

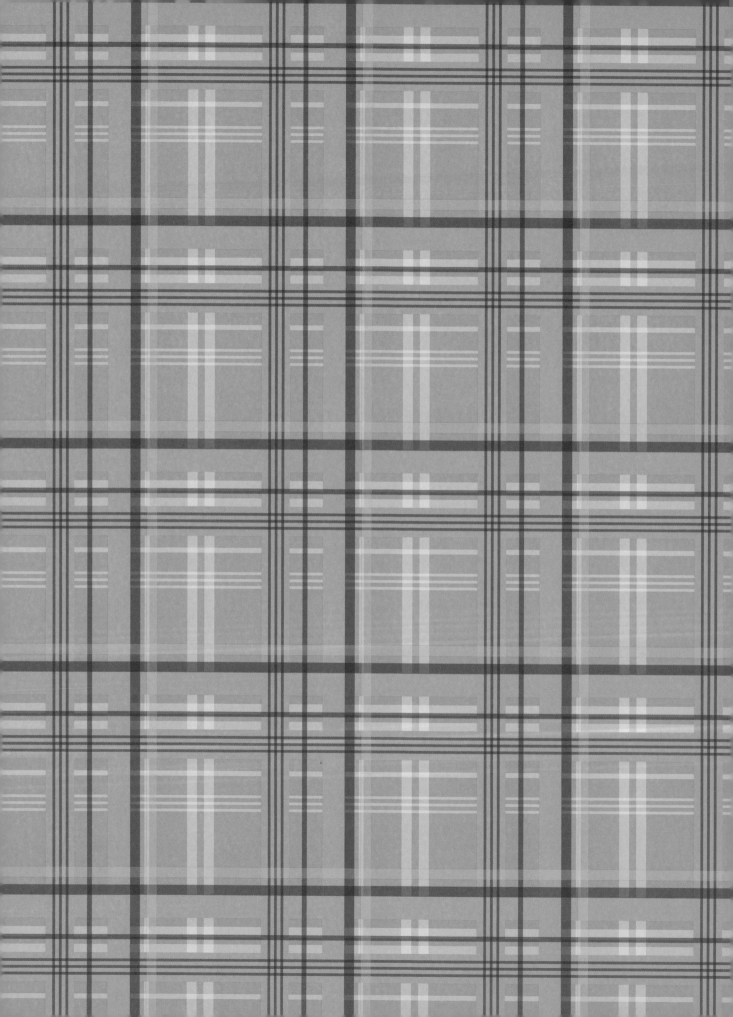

Fish and Shellfish

Fish of the West Indies

1. glasseye snapper
2. yellowtail snapper
3. rock beauty angelfish
4. blue runner
5. Spanish hogfish
6. land crabs
7. mahi mahi
8. conch
9. octopus
10. blue parrotfish
11. spiny lobster (crayfish)
12. spiny lobster (crayfish)
13. land crabs
14. queen triggerfish
15. mackerel
16. cardinalfish
17. trunkfish
18. coney
19. surgeonfish
20. pink parrotfish
21. Caesar grunt
22. red hind
23. red snapper
24. salt cod

2

3

4

5

6

7

8

9

10

11

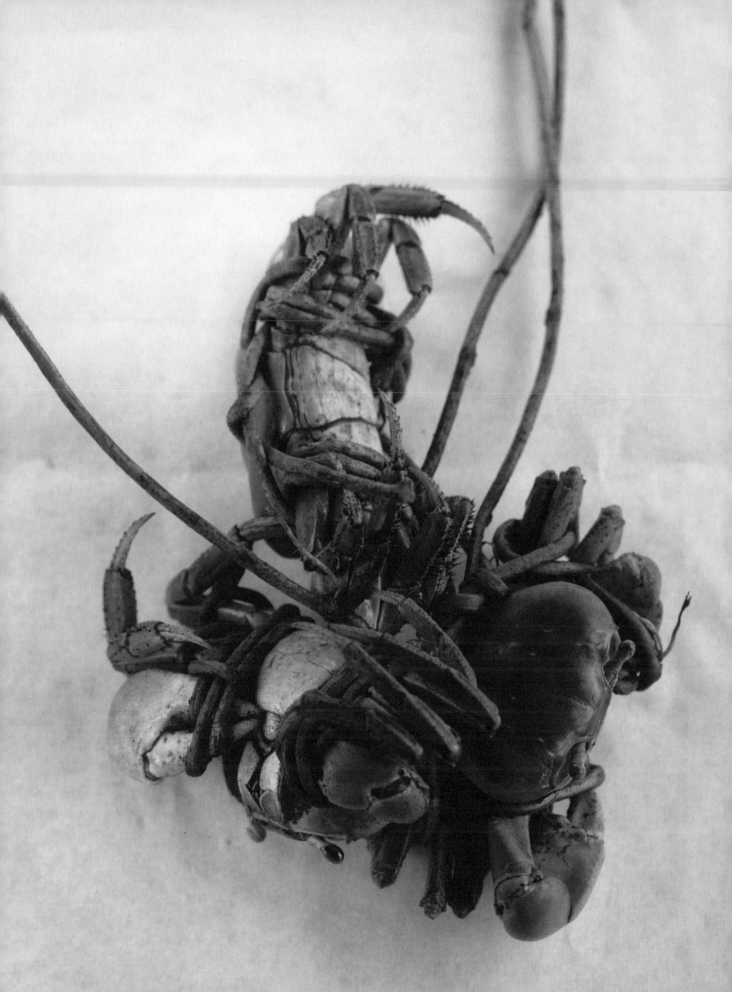

15

16

17

18

19

20

21

22

23

Babette's salt cod acras

Serves 4
Soak: 24 hours
Prep: 15 minutes
Chill: 24 hours
Cook: 10 minutes

14 oz (400 g) salt cod

----

11 oz (300 g) all-purpose
(plain) flour

----

1 cup (250 ml/ fl oz)
whole (full-cream) milk

----

1 sprig flat-leaf parsley,
chopped

----

2 scallions (spring
onions), chopped

----

1 onion, chopped

----

4 cloves garlic, chopped

----

salt and black pepper

¼ Scotch bonnet chile*
(chilli), chopped

----

2 teaspoons baking powder

----

8 cups (2 litres/3½ pints)
sunflower oil, for
deep-frying

Two days before serving, place the salt cod in
a large bowl of cool water to soak overnight. The
next day, place the cod in a saucepan of water to
cover and boil vigorously over high heat. Drain
the water and repeat several times. When the fish
is completely rehydrated, drain and break it into
pieces. Purée the fish pieces in a blender or
food processor.

Using a wooden spoon, mix the flour and milk in
a large bowl. Stir in the puréed cod, the parsley,
scallions, onion and garlic. Season to taste with
salt and pepper. Add the finely chopped chile. Stir
vigorously and refrigerate for 24 hours.

Taste the mixture 10 minutes before cooking the
acras*, to ensure that it is well salted. Mix in
the baking powder and stir well.

Heat the oil in a deep-fryer or large saucepan.
When very hot, drop in teaspoonfuls of the mixture
and fry until golden. The acras will take shape
and rise to the surface of the oil. Remove from
oil, drain on paper towels and serve hot.

Prawn acras

Serves 8
Prep: 15 minutes
Stand: 30 minutes
Cook: 5 minutes

1 lb 2 oz (500 g) Dublin
Bay prawns (if unavailable,
substitute jumbo shrimp)
----
scant 1 cup (200 g/7 oz)
all-purpose (plain) flour
----
1 sprig flat-leaf parsley,
finely chopped
----
3 scallions (spring
onions), finely chopped
----
1 shallot, finely chopped
----
1 clove garlic

¼ Scotch bonnet chile*
(chilli), finely chopped
----
1 teaspoon baking powder
----
4 cups (1 litre/1¾ pints)
sunflower oil, for
deep-frying
----
salt and black pepper

Shell and devein the prawns, removing the heads.

In a large bowl, mix the flour with 1 cup (250 ml/
8 fl oz) water. Stir in the parsley, scallion,
shallot, garlic and chile, to form a smooth paste.
Season to taste with salt and pepper.

Immediately add the baking powder and the prawns.
Mix well and set aside for 30 minutes.

Heat the oil in a deep-fryer or large saucepan.
When very hot, drop in teaspoonfuls of the mixture
and fry until golden. The acras* will take shape
and rise to the surface of the oil. Remove from
oil, drain on paper towels and serve hot.

Crispy salt cod parcels

Serves 4
Soak: 24 hours
Prep: 15 minutes
Cook: 10 minutes
Bake: 10 minutes

14 oz (400 g) salt cod
----
2 tablespoons sunflower
oil, plus additional
for brushing
----
1 shallot, finely chopped
----
2 cloves garlic,
finely chopped
----
1 sprig flat-leaf parsley,
finely chopped

½ bird's-eye chile*
(chilli), finely chopped
(if unavailable,
substitute piquin or
serrano chile)
----
4 scallions (spring
onions) or 8 chives,
finely chopped
----
2 large tomatoes, diced
salt and black pepper
----
4 sheets phyllo dough
(filo pastry)
----
1 scallion (spring onion),
quartered lengthwise,
blanched, for tying
bundles

The day before serving, place the salt cod in a large bowl of cool water to soak overnight.

The next day, place the cod in a saucepan of water and boil vigorously over high heat. Drain the water and repeat several times. When the fish is completely rehydrated, drain and break it into pieces. Preheat oven to 400°F (200°C/gas 6).

Heat the oil in a skillet or frying pan. When hot, add the shallot, garlic, parsley, chile, scallions and tomatoes. Fry gently for 10 minutes. Add the salt cod pieces. Season to taste with salt and pepper. Mix well and the filling is ready.

Brush each sheet of phyllo with oil and fold into a 6-inch (15 cm) square; place 1 tablespoon of filling at the center of each square. Fold up the edges of the pastry and gather together at the top. If desired, wrap and tie the bundles closed with blanched scallion 'strings'. Bake for 10 minutes. Serve hot.

Spicy parcels

Serves 4
Prep: 15 minutes
Cook: 10 minutes
Bake: 10 minutes

16 Dublin Bay prawns
(if unavailable, substitute
jumbo shrimp)
----
1 tablespoon olive oil,
plus additional for
brushing
----
10 basil leaves,
finely chopped
----
1 sprig flat-leaf parsley,
finely chopped
----
1 shallot, finely chopped
----
1 clove garlic,
finely chopped
----
1 zucchini (courgette),
diced
----
1 red bell pepper
(red pepper), diced

¼ bird's-eye chile*
(chilli), finely chopped
(if unavailable,
substitute piquin or
serrano chile)
----
salt and black pepper
----
4 sheets phyllo dough
(filo pastry)
----
1 scallion (spring onion),
quartered lengthwise,
blanched, for tying
bundles

Preheat oven to 400°F (200°C/gas 6). Shell and devein the prawns, removing the heads, and coarsely chop them. Set aside.

Heat the olive oil in a skillet or frying pan over low heat and gently fry the herbs, shallot and garlic without letting them brown. Add the prawns, zucchini, red bell pepper and chile. Season to taste with salt and pepper. Cook for 5 minutes.

Brush each sheet of phyllo with oil and fold into a 6-inch (15-cm) square; place 1 tablespoon of filling at the center of each square. Fold up the edges of the pastry and gather together at the top. If desired, wrap and tie the bundles closed with blanched scallion 'strings'. Bake for 10 minutes. Serve hot.

Deep-fried spicy calamari

Serves 4
Prep: 20 minutes
Cook: 3 minutes

1¾ lb (800 g) squid

----

scant ½ cup (100 g/3½ oz)
all-purpose (plain) flour

----

1 teaspoon cayenne pepper

----

salt and black pepper

----

4 cups (1 litre/1¾ pint)
sunflower oil, for
deep-frying

Clean the squid well. Remove the heads and finely slice the flesh into rings (calamari). Set aside.

In a large bowl, mix the flour and the cayenne pepper. Season to taste with salt and pepper. Dip the calamari rings in the flour mixture.

Heat the oil in a deep-fat fryer or large saucepan. When very hot, immerse the floured calamari rings. Fry until golden then remove and drain on paper towels. Serve hot.

Mini fish skewers with wasabi

Serves 4
Marinate: 8 hours
Prep: 10 minutes
Cook: 5 minutes

1 quantity Fish Marinade
(page 242)

1¾ lb (800 g) swordfish

----

juice of 2 limes

----

juice of 1 orange

¼ bird's-eye chile*
(chilli) (if unavailable,
substitute piquin or
serrano chile)

----

5 teaspoons wasabi powder

----

1 shallot, coarsely chopped

----

a few sprigs flat-leaf
parsley, chopped

----

2 tablespoons peanut
(groundnut) oil

----

salt and black pepper

The day before serving, cut the swordfish into large
dice and marinate in the refrigerator overnight.

The next day, drain the fish pieces and thread onto
skewers, allowing 2 skewers per person.

Purée the lime and orange juices, the chile, wasabi
and shallot in a blender or food processor, then
pour into a large bowl. Add the parsley and the
oil. Season to taste with salt and pepper and
set aside.

Preheat the broiler or grill and cook the skewers
for about 5 minutes, turning frequently so they
cook on all sides.

Top with the reserved sauce. If desired, serve with
a small green salad dressed with a lime vinaigrette.

Three-fish parcels

Serves 4
Prep: 20 minutes
Bake: 10 minutes

juice of 1 lime

1½ tablespoons coarsely
chopped fresh ginger

----

2 sprigs cilantro
(coriander)

----

2 cloves garlic,
coarsely chopped

3½ oz (100 g) goatfish
(red mullet) fillets

3½ oz (100 g) snapper
fillets

3½ oz (100 g) mahi mahi
fillets

----

2 tablespoons olive oil,
plus additional for
brushing

----

salt and black pepper

----

4 sheets phyllo dough
(filo pastry)

----

1 scallion (spring onion),
quartered lengthwise,
blanched, for tying bundles

Preheat oven to 400°F (200°C/gas 6). In a blender
or food processor, blend the lime juice, ginger,
cilantro and garlic.

Carefully remove the bones from the fish fillets.
Slice finely and place in a bowl. Pour the olive
oil over the fish and season with salt and pepper.
Add the lime juice mixture and mix well.

Brush each sheet of phyllo with oil and fold into
a 6-inch (15 cm) square; place one-quarter of the
filling at the center of each square. Fold up the
edges of the pastry and gather together at the top.
If desired, wrap and tie the bundles closed with
blanched scallion 'strings'. Bake for 10 minutes.
Serve hot.

Crispy parcels with a spicy sauce

Serves 4
Prep: 20 minutes
Cook: 10 minutes
Bake: 10 minutes

1¾ lb (800 g)
Dublin Bay prawns
(if unavailable,
substitute jumbo shrimp)
----
2 sprigs thyme
----
2 tablespoons sunflower
oil, plus additional
for brushing
----
3 scallions (spring
onions), chopped
----
1 sprig fresh basil,
chopped
----
1 clove garlic, chopped
----
salt and black pepper
----
juice of 1 lime
----
4 sheets phyllo dough
(filo pastry)
----
a few baby spinach leaves
----
1 scallion (spring onion),
quartered lengthwise,
blanched, for tying bundles

Preheat oven to 350°F (180°C/gas 4). Shell and devein the prawns, removing the heads, then slice finely. Set aside.

Pick the leaves off the fresh thyme sprigs and discard the stems.

Heat the oil in a skillet or frying pan. Fry the prawns to sear them, stirring constantly. Add the thyme, scallions, basil, garlic and cook for 2 minutes. Season to taste with salt and pepper. Add the lime juice. Mix well then remove from heat and set aside to cool.

Brush each sheet of phyllo with oil and fold into a 6-inch (15-cm) square; place a few baby spinach leaves at the center of each square, then add 2 tablespoons of the filling. Fold up the edges of the pastry and gather together at the top. If desired, wrap and tie the bundles closed with blanched scallion 'strings'. Bake for 10 minutes, until the parcels are crisp. Serve hot.

Crayfish-tail fritters with seafood cream

Serves 4
Prep: 30 minutes
Cook: 2 minutes

scant 1 cup (200 g/7 oz)
all-purpose (plain) flour

----

1 teaspoon baking powder

----

2 tablespoons olive oil

----

1 egg, beaten

----

1 bird's-eye chile*
(chilli), finely chopped
(if unavailable,
substitute piquin or
serrano chile)

----

pinch ground turmeric

----

3 oz (80 g) crabmeat

----

3 oz (80 g) cockles*
(if unavailable, substitute
hard-shell clams, such as
littlenecks or
cherrystones)

----

3 oz (80 g) Dublin Bay
prawns, finely chopped
(if unavailable, substitute
jumbo shrimp)

----

juice of 1 lime

----

salt and black pepper

----

4 cups (1 litre/1¾ pints)
sunflower oil, for
deep-frying

----

3 oz (80 g) crayfish tails

To prepare the batter, mix the flour, baking
powder, salt to taste and 1 tablespoon of the olive
oil. Thin down with ½ cup (125 ml/ 5 fl oz) warm
water and add the beaten egg. The batter should be
thick but runny. Finely chop the chile and add to
the batter. Set aside.

To prepare the seafood cream, bring 2 cups (500ml/
18 fl oz) water to the boil. Add the crabmeat,
cockles and prawns, season with salt and pepper,
and cook for 10 minutes over medium heat. Strain,
and set aside. Place the remaining tablespoon of
olive oil with the turmeric and cooked seafood in
a blender or food processor. Pour in the lime
juice. Season lightly with salt and pepper. Blend
for 1 to 2 minutes to form a smooth cream.

Heat the oil in a deep-fat fryer or large saucepan
until very hot. Immerse the crayfish tails in the
batter, then in the oil. Fry until brown then drain
on paper towels. Serve hot with the seafood cream.

Shredded salt cod on a cucumber salad

Serves 6
Soak: 20 minutes
Prep: 20 minutes
Chill: 1 hour

1¼ lb (600 g) salt cod

----

1 sprig flat-leaf parsley,
chopped, plus additional
for garnish

----

2 cloves garlic, chopped

----

3 scallions (spring
onions), chopped

----

3 chives, snipped, plus
additional for garnish

----

2 shallots, finely sliced

¼ Scotch bonnet chile*
(chilli), chopped

----

2 onions, finely sliced

----

3 tablespoons sunflower oil

----

juice of 2 limes

----

2 tablespoons white-wine
vinegar

----

salt and black pepper

----

1 cucumber, peeled
and sliced

Immerse the salt cod in hot water and let soak to
rehydrate for 5 minutes. Drain and repeat three
times. Drain the fish and set aside to cool on
paper towels. Remove the skin and bones from the
fish and shred the flesh with your fingers. Place
in a large bowl.

Add the parsley, 1 clove of the garlic, and the
scallions, chives, shallots, chile and onions.
Mix well. Stir in 2 tablespoons of the oil, the
juice of 1 of the limes, and 1 tablespoon of the
white-wine vinegar. Refrigerate for 1 hour.

Prepare a vinaigrette by mixing the remaining
garlic, lime juice, white-wine vinegar and oil,
seasoning to taste with salt and pepper. Pour the
vinaigrette over the cucumber slices. Arrange on a
serving plate. Top with the shredded cod. Garnish
with additional parsley and chives and, if desired,
serve with a green salad.

Crispy crab and lobster with vegetarian chile

Serves 4
Prep: 20 minutes
Cook: 15 minutes
Bake: 10 to 15 minutes

1 tablespoon olive oil
----
1 shallot, finely chopped
----
1 vegetarian chile*
(chilli), finely chopped
----
1 tablespoon garlic
infused vinegar

½ lb (200 g) crabmeat
----
1 lobster tail, flesh
weighing 11 oz/300 g when
removed from the shell,
cut into not-too-thick
segments
----
salt and black pepper
----
4 sheets phyllo dough
(filo pastry)
----
2 tablespoons (25 g/1 oz)
melted butter
----
1 quantity Spicy Sweet and
Sour Sauce (page 236)

Heat the oil in a skillet or frying pan and gently fry the shallot and chile. Allow them to brown slightly then add the vinegar, crabmeat and lobster segments. Mix well. Season to taste with salt and pepper and cook for 2 minutes over medium heat. Remove from heat and set aside to cool.

Preheat oven to 350°F (180°C/gas 4). Brush one side of each sheet of phyllo with melted butter then place 2 tablespoons of filling in the middle of each. Fold the pastry into small square parcels. Bake for 10 to 15 minutes until the parcels are well browned. Serve hot with Spicy Sweet and Sour Sauce.

Banana flowers stuffed with seafood

Serves 6
Prep: 15 minutes
Cook: 10 minutes

1 banana flower

----

12 basil leaves, chopped

----

1 shallot

----

12 cilantro (coriander)
leaves, chopped

----

1 clove garlic, chopped

----

6 scallions (spring
onions), chopped

----

juice of 1 lemon

----

4 tablespoons olive oil

----

1 cup (250 g/ 9 oz) mixed
seafood such as cockles*,
clams, squid, and prawns,
chopped

----

salt and black pepper

----

2 tablespoons white-wine
vinegar

----

juice of 1 lime

2½ oz (60 g) crushed
peanuts

----

1 tablespoon clear honey

----

1 ripe banana, sliced

----

6 chives

----

1 quantity Spicy Sweet and
Sour Sauce (page 236)

Remove 6 petals from the banana flower and set
aside. Chop the remaining petals. Mix together the
basil, shallot, cilantro, garlic, scallions, and
lemon juice.

Heat the oil in a heavy-based saucepan and gently
fry the herb-garlic mixture. Add the chopped banana
flower and the seafood. Season to taste with salt
and pepper. Add the vinegar and cook over low heat
for 5 minutes. Stir regularly and gently. Remove
from heat, add the lime juice, crushed peanuts and
the honey and mix well. The filling is ready.

Blanch the 6 whole banana flower petals by immersing
them in lightly salted hot water for a few seconds.
Place 1 tablespoon of filling in the middle of each
petal, add the sliced banana, then roll up and tie
with a chive that has been softened in steam.
Serve warm with Spicy Sweet and Sour Sauce, with
optional lightly steamed scallions and cilantro.

Seafood bake with lemongrass

Serves 4
Prep: 20 minutes
Cook: 25 minutes
Bake: 15 minutes

3 sprigs flat-leaf parsley

----

1 sprig thyme

----

1 stalk lemongrass, cut
into 1 in (2.5 cm) pieces

----

2 white onions, chopped

----

2 cloves garlic, chopped

----

pinch chili powder

3½ oz (100 g)
Mediterranean prawns
(if unavailable,
substitute jumbo shrimp)

3½ oz (100 g) whelks

----

6 clams

----

5 oz (150 g) lobster tail

3½ oz (100 g) swordfish
fillets

----

sunflower oil, for frying

----

salt and black pepper

¼ cup (50 g/2 oz) all-
purpose (plain) flour

----

5 oz (150 ml/¼ pint) light
(single) cream

----

2 eggs

¼ cup (50 g/2 oz)
grated Parmesan

Mix the parsley, thyme, lemongrass, onions and
garlic in a blender or food processor. Add the
chili powder. Set aside.

Shell and devein the prawns, removing the heads.
Cook the whelks then remove from shells and clean.
In a heavy-based saucepan, cook the clams in a
little hot water until they open. Remove from
shells and set aside, retaining the cooking water.
Shell the lobster tails. Finely dice all the
seafood, including the swordfish.

Heat the oil in a skillet or frying pan over high
heat and fry the herb mixture. Add the seafood.
Cook for 3 minutes over medium heat. Season to
taste with salt and pepper. Remove from heat and
set aside.

In a bowl, vigorously beat the flour, cream and
eggs. Set aside.

Preheat oven to 400°F (200°C/gas 6). Grease a
baking dish. Pour in the seafood mixture, top with
the cream sauce and sprinkle with the Parmesan.
Bake for 15 minutes. Serve hot.

Baked mirlitons with spicy honey crab

Serves 4
Prep: 30 minutes
Cook: 30 minutes
Bake: 10 minutes

2 mirlitons* (chayotes)
----
1 tablespoon sunflower oil
----
1 shallot, finely chopped
----
1 basil leaf, finely
chopped
----
1 sprig flat-leaf parsley,
finely chopped
----
1 clove garlic, finely
chopped
----
2 scallions (spring
onions)

½ lb (200 g) crabmeat
----
1 tablespoon clear honey
----
salt and black pepper
----
1 Scotch bonnet chile*
(chilli)
----
1 to 2 tablespoons
breadcrumbs, plus
additional for sprinkling

¼ cup (50 g)
grated Parmesan

Cut the mirlitons in half lengthwise and cook them in 4 cups (1 litre/1¾ pints) of simmering water for 20 minutes. Drain and set aside to cool.

Using a teaspoon, remove the flesh from each half without breaking the skin. Set the skins aside. Purée the flesh in a blender or food processor.

Heat the oil in a heavy-based saucepan over high heat. Add the shallot, basil, parsley, garlic and scallions and fry until lightly browned. Stir in the crabmeat, the puréed mirlitons and the honey; mix well. Season to taste with salt and pepper. Add the chile and cook for 2 to 3 minutes. If the filling is too runny, add breadcrumbs as needed, mixing well to form a smooth paste.

Preheat oven to 400°F (200°C/gas 6). Stuff each reserved mirliton shell with filling, sprinkle with Parmesan and breadcrumbs, if desired, then bake for 10 minutes. Serve hot.

Large clams stuffed Creole-style

Serves 6
Prep: 20 minutes
Cook: 10 minutes
Bake: 10 minutes

3½ oz (100 g) stale bread

---

2 cups (500 ml/18 fl oz)
whole (full-cream) milk

---

12 large clams

---

1 sprig cilantro
(coriander)

---

1 sprig thyme

---

1 shallot, chopped

---

1 sprig flat-leaf parsley

---

1 clove garlic

---

4 teaspoons (20 g/¾ oz)
butter

---

salt and black pepper

---

1 Scotch bonnet chile*
(chilli), chopped

---

juice of 2 limes

---

2 tablespoons breadcrumbs

Soak the stale bread in the milk. Meanwhile, wash the clams in plenty of water, scrubbing the shells until they are completely clean. Place in a heavy-based saucepan with 1 cup (250 ml/8 fl oz) water and bring to a boil for 5 to 6 minutes until the shells open, then set aside to cool.

Remove the clams from their shells and finely chop the flesh; set aside. Squeeze the bread to remove the milk. In a blender or food processor, chop the cilantro, thyme, shallot, parsley and garlic; set aside. Then purée the bread and set aside.

Melt the butter in a heavy-based saucepan over medium heat and gently fry the herb mixture for 2 to 3 minutes. Add the chopped clam flesh and the puréed bread, mixing well with a wooden spoon. Season lightly with salt and pepper. Add the chile and the lime juice. Cook over low heat for 5 minutes, stirring constantly. The filling is ready.

Preheat oven to 350°F (180°C/gas 4). Stuff each clam shell with the filling, sprinkle with breadcrumbs and bake for 10 minutes. Serve hot.

Shredded cod layers with avocado cream

Serves 4
Soak: 24 hours
Prep: 40 minutes
Cook: 10 minutes

1 lb 2 oz (500 g) salt cod
----
2 Scotch bonnet chiles*
(chillis)
----
2 sprigs flat-leaf
parsley, finely chopped
----
2 sprigs thyme, leaves
removed and finely chopped
----
2 white onions, finely
chopped
----
1 clove garlic, finely
chopped
----
1 scallion (spring onion),
finely chopped
----
3 tablespoons olive oil
----
4 limes
----
salt and black pepper
----
1 cucumber, skin on, cut
in thick slices
----
2 avocados

Place the salt cod in a large bowl of cool water to soak overnight.

The next day, place the cod in a saucepan of water and boil vigorously over high heat. Drain the water and repeat several times. When the fish is totally rehydrated, drain and shred the flesh with your fingers. Set aside.

Finely chop 1 of the chiles and combine with the parsley, thyme, onion, garlic, and scallion in a large bowl. Add 2 tablespoons of the oil, the juice of 3 of the limes and the shredded cod. Stir the mixture vigorously so that the herbs and spices permeate the fish. Season to taste with salt and pepper. Refrigerate.

When ready to serve, place a large round pastry cutter on a plate and line the bottom with a layer of cucumber. Spread with a layer of shredded cod, then another layer of cucumber. Continue adding layers until the pastry cutter is full. Finish with a layer of cucumber.

Blend the flesh of the avocados with the juice of the remaining lime, the remaining 1 tablespoon olive oil and the remaining chile. Place the filled pastry cutter onto or next to the avocado cream. Carefully remove the pastry cutter. Serve cold.

Ouassou mousse in eggshells

Serves 6
Prep: 30 minutes
Cook: 23 minutes

4 ouassous*
(if unavailable, substitute
large crayfish)
----
1 sprig cilantro
(coriander)
----
5 chives
----
1 clove garlic
----
2 shallots
----
1 tablespoon olive oil
----
2 teaspoons (10 g/¼ oz)
butter
----
pinch ground turmeric
----
pinch of chile (chilli)
powder
----
juice of 2 limes
----
salt and black pepper
----
2 tablespoons light
(single) cream
----
6 eggs
----
12 thin strips toasted
bread, rubbed with garlic

Fill a heavy-based saucepan with salted water,
bring to a vigorous boil over high heat and cook
the ouassous for 20 minutes. Shell the ouassous
and blend the flesh in a blender or food processor.
Set aside.

Purée the cilantro, chives, peeled garlic and
peeled shallots in a blender or food processor until
thick and creamy. Heat the oil with the butter in
a heavy-based saucepan. Stir in the blended herb
mixture, turmeric and the chile powder. Fry gently
over low heat for 2 to 3 minutes without browning.
Add the ouassou flesh and the lime juice and cook
for 2 minutes more. Season to taste with salt and
pepper. Mix well.

Remove from heat and add the cream. Purée the whole
mixture in a blender or food processor for a few
seconds to form a smooth mousse.

Break off the crown of the eggshells using a little
egg guillotine (or, if you don't have one, a small
saw). Empty each egg and reserve the empty shells.
Using a piping bag or a teaspoon, carefully fill
each eggshell with the hot mousse. Serve the eggshells in eggcups, accompanied by the toast strips.

Deep-fried shark batons with spicy mayonnaise

Serves 4
Prep: 20 minutes
Cook: 5 minutes

1 lb 2 oz (500 g) shark
fillets, finely sliced
----
scant ½ cup (100 g/3½ oz)
all-purpose (plain) flour
----
pinch cayenne pepper
----
salt and black pepper
----
4 cups (1 litre/1¾ pint)
sunflower oil, for
deep-frying

Spicy mayonnaise

1 egg yolk
----
1 tablespoon mustard
----
pinch cayenne pepper
----
1 cup (250 ml/8 fl oz)
sunflower oil
----
juice of 2 limes
----
2 cloves garlic, chopped
----
1 sprig cilantro
(coriander), chopped
----
salt and black pepper

First prepare the spicy mayonnaise: Place the egg
yolk in a large bowl with the mustard. Set aside
for a few minutes then add the cayenne pepper.
Slowly pour in the oil while whisking constantly.
Keep whisking gently until a mayonnaise forms. When
creamy, add the lime juice, garlic and cilantro.
Season to taste with salt and pepper. Mix well and
chill until ready to serve.

Place the flour, cayenne pepper, salt and pepper in
a bowl. Add the shark slices, mixing well to cover
each slice with flour.

Heat the oil in a large saucepan. Drop in the shark
slices and deep-fry until golden. Remove from oil
and drain on paper towels. Serve with the spicy
mayonnaise.

Crab profiteroles on a saffron seafood cream

Serves 6
Prep: 45 minutes
Cook: 15 minutes
Bake: 10 minutes

scant ½ cup (100 ml/3½ fl oz) whole (full-cream) milk

----

1 teaspoon salt

----

5 tablespoons (75 g/3 oz) butter

----

scant ½ cup (100 g/3½ oz) all-purpose (plain) flour

----

3 eggs

----

1 sprig flat-leaf parsley

----

1 bird's-eye chile* (chilli) (if unavailable, substitute piquin or serrano chile)

----

1 shallot

----

1 clove garlic

----

1 tablespoon sunflower oil

----

11 oz (300 g) crabmeat

----

salt and black pepper

----

1 quantity Saffron Seafood Cream (page 234)

To make the choux pastry, pour the milk and a scant ½ cup (100 ml/3½ fl oz) water into a saucepan. Add the salt and butter and bring to a boil, stirring constantly with a wooden spoon. Add the flour all at once and stir vigorously to form a smooth paste. Add 2 of the eggs, one at a time, making sure that each is incorporated completely. Continue stirring the pastry for 10 minutes then remove from heat and set aside.

Mix the parsley, chile, shallot and garlic in a blender or food processor. Heat the oil in a saucepan over low heat then gently fry the herb mixture for 2 minutes. Add the crabmeat and season to taste with salt and pepper. Cook for 3 minutes, stirring constantly.

Remove mixture from heat and purée in a blender or food processor, adding a little milk if it is too thick, and, if desired, a little additional chopped chile to form a lovely smooth cream. Set aside.

Preheat oven to 400°F (200°C/gas 6). Place the choux pastry in a piping bag with a smooth nozzle and line a baking sheet with baking paper. Pipe 24 balls of pastry onto the baking sheet. Beat the remaining egg and brush over each pastry ball. Bake for 10 minutes or until golden.

Arrange the pastry balls on a plate. Cut each one in half and fill with the crab purée. Serve with the Saffron Seafood Cream.

Raw small conch with lime and a sweet and sour sauce

Serves 6
Prep: 30 minutes
Chill: 2 hours

2 tablespoons white-wine
vinegar
----
8 limes

2¼ lb (1 kg)
small conch*
----
juice of 2 oranges

¼ cup (50 g/2 oz)
red bell peppers
(red peppers), diced

¼ cup (50 g/2 oz)
green bell peppers
(green peppers), diced

¼ (20 g/2 oz) of a small
zucchini (courgette), diced
----
2 sprigs cilantro
(coriander), chopped
----
1 sprig flat-leaf parsley,
chopped
----
pinch chili powder
----
salt and black pepper

Add the white-wine vinegar and the juice of 3 limes to a basin of water. Wash the conchs in this water until the skin becomes rough to the touch. If they still slide under the fingers, repeat the procedure. Once the conchs are clean, cut in half lengthwise. Using the point of a knife, scrape out the yellow part at the center of the flesh. Remove the black skin and the operculum at the end of each conch. Finely slice the conchs.

In a large bowl, thoroughly mix the conch slices, juice of remaining 5 limes, orange juice, red and green bell peppers, zucchini, cilantro, parsley and chili powder. Season lightly with salt and pepper. Refrigerate for 2 hours before serving.

Pan-fried camarons with sweet herbs and a star fruit jam

Serves 4
Prep: 15 minutes
Cook: 18 minutes

8 camarons*
(if unavailable,
substitute Dublin Bay
prawns or jumbo shrimp)
----
pinch cayenne pepper
----
2 tablespoons superfine
(caster) sugar
----
2 limes, peeled, seeded,
and diced
----
3 star fruit, diced
----
1 tablespoon peanut
(groundnut) oil
----
2 cloves garlic, finely
chopped
----
1 sprig dill, chopped
----
1 sprig chervil, chopped
----
1 sprig cilantro
(coriander), plus extra
to garnish
----
1 sprig flat-leaf parsley,
chopped
----
1 tablespoon cumin seeds,
crushed
----
salt and black pepper

Shell and devein the camarons, removing the heads.
Lightly score each camaron lengthwise starting at
the bottom and not touching the tip. Set aside.

In a saucepan, bring 1 cup (250 ml/8 fl oz) water,
the cayenne pepper and sugar to a boil, then add
the lime and the star fruit. Simmer over low heat
for 15 minutes. Purée the mixture in a blender or
food processor.

Heat the oil in a skillet or frying pan. Add the
camarons, garlic, herbs and cumin. Season to taste
with salt and pepper. Mix gently and brown well for
2 to 3 minutes. Serve hot with the star fruit jam.
Garnish with chopped cilantro.

Spicy stuffed West Indian crabs

Serves 6
Soak: 12 to 24 hours
Prep: 20 minutes
Cook: 35 minutes
Bake: 5 minutes

a few slices stale bread

----

9 oz (250 g) crabmeat or
enough whole crabs to
yield 9 oz (250 g) flesh

----

1 tablespoon sunflower oil

----

3 onions, finely chopped

----

2 cloves garlic, finely
chopped

----

1 shallot, finely chopped

----

2 sprigs flat-leaf
parsley, chopped

----

1 sprig thyme, leaves
removed and chopped

----

1 vegetarian chile*
(chilli), chopped

----

salt and black pepper

----

3 tablespoons breadcrumbs

Soak the stale bread in water overnight.

If you are preparing this dish from whole crabs,
the next day, wash and scrub the crabs then immerse
in a stock pot of vigorously boiling water. Cook
for 20 minutes. Drain and set aside to cool. Once
cool, shell the crabs and break up the flesh.
Remove the fat and cartilage from the crab shells
and retain everything.

Heat the oil in a heavy-based saucepan then lightly
fry the onions, garlic, shallot, parsley, thyme
and chile for 5 to 6 minutes. Season to taste with
salt and pepper. Squeeze the bread to remove the
water and add to the herb mixture. Bring to a
simmer and cook for 5 to 6 minutes, then add the
crabmeat along with the fat and cartilage. Mix well
and adjust the seasoning if desired. Simmer for 6
more minutes.

Preheat oven to 350°F (180°C/gas 4). Fill the crab
shells with the crab mixture and sprinkle with
breadcrumbs. Arrange on a baking sheet and bake for
5 minutes until brown. Serve hot.

Salt cod tartlets with coconut

Serves 6
Soak/Stand: 24 hours
Prep: 20 minutes
Cook: 10 minutes
Bake: 35 minutes

1¾ lb (800 g) salt cod

----

1 sprig flat-leaf parsley

----

1 sprig thyme, leaves
removed and chopped

----

1 sprig tarragon

----

2 shallots

----

2 cloves garlic

----

1 tablespoon olive oil

----

scant 1 cup (200 ml/
7 fl oz) coconut milk

----

1 tablespoon crème fraîche
(see below)

----

salt and black pepper

----

1 egg

----

1 roll puff (flaky) pastry

----

2 tablespoons breadcrumbs

¼ bird's-eye chile*
(chilli)

Crème fraîche

1 cup (250 ml/8 fl oz)
heavy (double) cream

----

2 tablespoons buttermilk

Place the salt cod in a large bowl of cool water to soak overnight.

The next day, place the cod in a saucepan of water and boil vigorously over high heat. Drain the water and repeat several times. When the fish is completely rehydrated, drain and break it into pieces. Purée the fish pieces in a blender or food processor. Add the parsley, thyme and tarragon, then the shallots and garlic. Blend and set aside.

Heat the oil in a large saucepan over medium heat. Add the cod mixture and cook for 2 to 3 minutes, stirring frequently to prevent sticking to the bottom of the pan. Mix in the coconut milk and crème fraîche (see below). Season to taste with salt and pepper. Simmer for 2 to 4 minutes. When there is no more liquid, add the egg and stir vigorously. Remove from heat.

Preheat oven to 400°F (200°C/gas 6). Grease and lightly flour six 4-inch tart pans. Fill them with pastry and prick the bottoms with a fork. Pour in the filling and sprinkle with breadcrumbs. Bake for 25 minutes then reduce the heat to 300°F (150°C/gas 2). Bake for 10 minutes more. Serve hot.

If you are unable to buy crème fraîche, you can make it as follows: in a small bowl, whisk together the heavy cream and buttermilk, blending thoroughly; set bowl in a larger bowl of hot water to bring cream to room temperature (about 70°F/20°C), then remove; partially cover and let stand 8 to 24 hours or until very thick; stir well; cover and refrigerate for up to 10 days.

Barbecued West Indian fish

Serves 4
Marinate: 8 hours
Prep: 20 minutes
Grill: 20 minutes

1 quantity Fish Marinade
(page 242)
----
4 whole mahi mahi or
4 whole snapper
----
3 tablespoons peanut
(groundnut) oil, plus
additional for brushing
----
juice of 4 limes
----
2 scallions (spring
onions), finely chopped
----
1 sprig thyme, leaves
finely chopped
----
1 sprig flat-leaf parsley,
finely chopped
----
1 sprig cilantro
(coriander), finely chopped
----
1 red onion, finely chopped
----
2 cloves garlic, finely
chopped
----
1 Scotch bonnet chile*
(chilli), finely chopped
----
salt and black pepper

The day before serving, scale the fish and marinate
in the refrigerator overnight.

The next day, remove the fish from the marinade and
dry using a clean cloth. Brush both sides with oil.
Barbecue the fish, preferably over wood charcoal,
for 10 minutes on each side.

Meanwhile, in a large bowl, combine the oil, lime
juice, the chopped herbs, onion, garlic and chile.
Season to taste with salt and pepper. Top the fish
with this sauce. Serve hot.

Ouassou blaff

Serves 4
Prep: 10 minutes
Cook: 25 minutes

2 sprigs thyme
----

flat-leaf parsley
----

4 scallions (spring
onions), sliced
----

salt and black pepper
----

3 bay leaves
----

2 tablespoons powdered
fish stock, or one fish
stock cube, crumbled
----

4 cloves garlic, chopped
----

5 medium-sized white
onions, chopped
----

8 large ouassous*
(if unavailable, substitute
large crayfish)
----

5 limes
----

1 Scotch bonnet chile*
(chilli)
----

grated zest of 1 lemon

Heat 1 cup (250 ml/8 fl oz) water in a heavy-based saucepan over medium heat, then stir in the thyme, parsley and 1 of the scallions. Season to taste with salt and pepper. Add the bay leaves, powdered fish stock, garlic and onions. Bring to a boil.

Reduce the heat to low and simmer for 3 to 5 minutes, then add the ouassous, the juice of 3 of the limes and the whole chile. Cover and cook over medium heat for 20 minutes, stirring occasionally, taking care not to burst the chile.

Arrange the ouassous on a serving plate. Pass the sauce through a sieve. Adjust the seasoning if desired, then add the juice of the remaining 2 limes; if desired, add additional garlic and chile to taste. Pour this sauce over the ouassous and garnish the blaff* with the remaining scallions and the lemon zest.

Sea bream blaff

Serves 4
Marinate: 8 hours
Prep: 15 minutes
Cook: 8 minutes

1 quantity Fish Marinade
(page 242)
----
4 porgy (sea bream) steaks
----
2 cloves garlic, finely
chopped
----
4 scallions (spring
onions), finely chopped
----
2 white onions, thinly
sliced
----
1 bay leaf
----
1 sprig thyme, leaves
removed and chopped
----
2 whole cloves
----
1 sprig flat-leaf parsley,
finely chopped
----
salt and black pepper
----
1 Scotch bonnet chile*
(chilli)
----
2 tablespoons sunflower oil
----
juice of 4 limes

Clean the fish steaks and marinate in the
refrigerator overnight.

The next day, pour 1 cup (250 ml/8 fl oz) water
into a large saucepan then stir in half of the
chopped garlic, scallions, onions, bay leaf, thyme,
cloves and parsley. Season to taste with salt and
pepper. Heat for 3 minutes, then add the fish and
the whole chile; simmer for 5 minutes.

Remove from heat and add the oil, lime juice and
the remaining garlic. Mix well, taking care not
to burst the chile. Serve the blaff* hot.

Sea urchin blaff

Serves 6
Prep: 10 minutes
Cook: 10 minutes

24 sea urchins
----
3 tablespoons sunflower oil
----
1 shallot, finely chopped
----
3 cloves garlic, finely
chopped
----
6 chives, chopped
----
salt and black pepper
----
2 sprigs flat-leaf
parsley, finely chopped
----
1 sprig thyme, finely
chopped
----
1 Scotch bonnet chile*
(chilli)
----
juice of 3 limes

Ask your fishmonger to open the sea urchins for
you. Remove the yellow ovaries with a teaspoon
and retain.

Heat the oil in a high-sided skillet or frying pan.
Gently fry the shallot, garlic, chives, parsley and
thyme, season with salt and pepper if desired, then
add the sea urchin ovaries. Continue cooking over
medium heat for 2 to 3 minutes, taking care that
nothing sticks to the pan.

Cover with 1 cup (250 ml/8 fl oz) water. Add the
whole chile, taking care that it does not burst.
Cook for 5 minutes more. Finish by adding the lime
juice. Serve the blaff* immediately. If desired,
serve in urchin half shells.

Blaff of snapper steaks marinated in lime and a yam purée

Serves 4
Marinate: 8 hours
Prep: 10 minutes
Cook: 10 minutes

1 quantity Fish Marinade
(page 242)
----
4 snapper steaks
----
3 white onions, finely
sliced
----
1 sprig thyme, leaves
removed
----
1 sprig flat-leaf parsley,
finely chopped
----
3 cloves garlic, finely
chopped
----
3 bay leaves
----
1 Scotch bonnet chile*
(chilli)
----
salt and black pepper
----
juice of 4 limes
----
1 tablespoon sunflower oil
----
1 quantity Yam Purée
(page 224)

Scale and clean the snapper and marinate in the refrigerator overnight.

The next day, pour 1 cup (250 ml/8 fl oz) water into a heavy-based saucepan and add the onions, thyme, parsley, 1 clove chopped garlic, bay leaves and whole chile. Bring to a boil and cook for 10 minutes.

Drain the snapper and add to the pan. Season with salt and pepper. Cook over medium heat for 10 minutes more. Remove from heat then add the lime juice, the remaining chopped garlic and the oil. Mix well and serve the blaff* hot with the Yam Purée on the side.

West Indian-style swordfish in white sauce

Serves 4
Stand: 8 to 24 hours
Prep: 10 minutes
Cook: 15 minutes

1¾ lb (800 g) swordfish
fillets

---

2 shallots, peeled, whole

---

2 onions, peeled, whole

---

2 cloves garlic, peeled,
whole

---

1 sprig thyme

---

1 sprig flat-leaf parsley,
chopped

---

2 scallions (spring
onions), chopped

---

2 bay leaves

---

salt and black pepper

---

2 tablespoons (30g/1 oz)
butter

---

2 tablespoons all-purpose
(plain) flour, sifted

---

1 egg

---

2 tablespoons crème
fraîche (see page 62)

---

2 limes

---

1 Scotch bonnet chile*
(chilli), finely chopped

The day before serving, make the crème fraîche
and let stand 8 to 24 hours or until very thick.
(The crème fraîche will keep, covered, in the
refrigerator for up to 10 days.)

The next day, place the swordfish fillets in a
saucepan. Cover with water then add the shallots,
onions, garlic, thyme and parsley. Add the
scallions and bay leaves. Season to taste with
salt and pepper. Bring to a boil then simmer over
very low heat for 5 minutes.

Remove the fish from the water and continue cooking
the stock for 3 to 4 minutes. Pass through a sieve
and set aside.

In another saucepan, melt the butter and stir
in the flour. When the mixture starts to bubble,
slowly add the fish stock, stirring constantly.
Cook for 2 to 3 minutes.

Beat the egg vigorously in a bowl; stir in the
crème fraîche. Pour the egg mixture into the
thickened stock and stir until fully incorporated.
Add the juice of the limes and the finely chopped
chile. Pour this sauce over the fish.

Swordfish strips with lime-marinated mangoes and coconut

Serves 4
Marinate: 7 hours
Prep: 30 minutes

1 coconut

----

1 lb 2 oz (500 g)
swordfish fillets,
skin removed

----

6 limes

----

1 sprig flat-leaf parsley,
chopped

----

6 basil leaves, chopped

----

1 bunch cilantro
(coriander), chopped

----

1 Scotch bonnet chile*
(chilli), chopped

----

2 tablespoons balsamic
vinegar

----

2 tablespoons acacia-tree
honey

----

2 tablespoons olive oil

----

pinch ground cinnamon

----

salt and black pepper

----

1 cup (250 g/9 oz) mixed
salad greens (leaves)

----

2 mangoes, peeled and cut
into strips

Break open the coconut and grate the flesh.
Pour 1 cup (250 ml/8 fl oz) hot water over the
grated coconut and let stand until the water is
completely cooled.

Meanwhile, finely slice the swordfish fillets into
rounds and then into strips. Place the strips on a
plate or in a shallow dish. Using your hand, roll
the limes on the work surface then cut them in half
lengthwise. If desired, set aside a few slices for
use as a garnish; squeeze the rest and pour the
juice over the swordfish. Marinate in the
refrigerator for 2 hours.

Place the cooled coconut flesh in a clean cloth
and squeeze to remove as much liquid as possible.
Pour all the liquid over the marinated swordfish
strips. Reserve a little parsley and cilantro for
garnish, then add the remaining parsley and basil,
the cilantro and chile to the fish. Season to taste
with salt and pepper. Mix well then refrigerate
for 5 hours.

Combine the balsamic vinegar with the honey, then
add the olive oil and the cinnamon. Season to taste
with salt and pepper, mix well and heat gently.
Remove from heat, allow to cool slightly, add the
salad greens and stir carefully.

Arrange the salad on a plate, add the drained
swordfish strips and the mangoes. Sprinkle with
chopped parsley and cilantro. Garnish with a few
thin lime slices if desired.

Sea bream fillets with garlic and a passionfruit cream

Serves 4
Marinate: 8 hours
Prep: 10 minutes
Cook: 20 minutes

1 quantity Fish Marinade
(page 242)

----

4 porgy (sea bream)
fillets

----

2 tablespoons peanut
(groundnut) oil

----

4 cloves garlic, crushed

----

salt and black pepper

----

6 passionfruit

----

1 bird's-eye chile*
(chilli) (if unavailable,
substitute piquin or
serrano chile)

----

1 sprig cilantro
(coriander), chopped

----

1 tablespoon honey

----

2 limes

----

2 chives, finely chopped

Clean the fish fillets and marinate in the refrigerator overnight.

The next day, drain the fillets, dry them with a clean cloth and set aside. Heat the oil in a non-stick skillet or frying pan and gently fry the garlic. (If you don't have a non-stick pan, lightly flour each fish fillet before placing in the hot oil.) When the oil is very hot, fry the fish fillets skin-side down to sear the flesh. Season to taste with salt and pepper and cook over medium heat for 5 minutes on each side. Remove from heat and set aside.

Place the pulp of the passionfruit (including the seeds) in a blender or food processor with a scant ½ cup (100 ml/3½ fl oz) water. Add the chile and blend for 2 to 3 minutes. Pass the purée through a sieve. Add the chopped cilantro and pour into a saucepan. Simmer over low heat for about 4 minutes. Add the honey and the juice of 1 of the limes.

Serve each fish fillet with 2 tablespoons of the passionfruit sauce. Sprinkle with chives and the juice of the remaining lime. Serve hot.

Crispy snapper fillets in a giraumon sauce

Serves 4
Prep: 15 minutes
Cook: 10 minutes

5 tablespoons sunflower oil

----

11 oz (300 g) giraumon*,
peeled and diced (if
unavailable, substitute
another variety of pumpkin)

----

3 large tomatoes, peeled
and diced

----

4 cloves garlic, finely
chopped

1½ tablespoons finely
chopped fresh ginger

----

1 stalk lemongrass, finely
chopped

----

1 vegetarian chile*
(chilli), finely chopped

----

salt and black pepper

----

2 teaspoons superfine
(caster) sugar

2¼ lb (1 kg) snapper
fillets, skin on

----

1 lime

Heat 2 tablespoons of the oil in a large saucepan.
Add the giraumon, tomatoes, garlic, ginger,
lemongrass and chile. Cover and cook over low
heat for 10 minutes. Add a little water during
cooking if necessary.

Remove from heat and purée in a blender or food
processor. Season to taste with salt and pepper.
Add the sugar and mix well. Keep warm.

Cut the snapper fillets into large pieces. Season
to taste with salt and pepper. Heat the remaining
3 tablespoons oil in a skillet or frying pan until
very hot then fry the snapper fillets skin-side
down for 2 to 3 minutes to sear the flesh. Turn
over and cook for 1 to 2 minutes more. Cut the lime
into quarters and squeeze over the fish.

Serve the snapper fillets bathed in the creamy
giraumon sauce and, if desired, garnish with finely
chopped herbs and fried thin slices of garlic.

West Indian-style lobster fricassee stuffed with tomatoes

Serves 4
Prep: 10 minutes
Cook: 20 minutes

2¼ lb (1 kg) young
lobsters or lobster tails,
shells on, cut into good-
size segments
----
3 tablespoons peanut
(groundnut) oil
----
3 sprigs thyme, finely
chopped
----
1 sprig cilantro
(coriander), finely chopped
----
1 sprig flat-leaf parsley,
finely chopped
----
1 shallot, finely chopped
----
3 very ripe tomatoes, diced
----
2 bay leaves
----
1 Scotch bonnet chile*
(chilli)
----
2 tablespoons tomato purée
----
1 tablespoon fish bouillon
granules (powdered fish
stock or 1 fish stock
cube, crumbled)
----
4 limes
----
salt and black pepper
----
2 cloves garlic, chopped
----
1 teaspoon cornstarch
(cornflour)

Heat the oil in a heavy-based saucepan and gently
fry the thyme, cilantro, parsley, shallot and
tomatoes. Add the bay leaves, reduce the heat to
low and simmer for 5 minutes, stirring very gently
with a wooden spoon.

Stir in the lobster pieces then add water to just
cover. Add the whole chile, the tomato purée, the
bouillon mixed with a little water, and the juice
of 3 of the limes. Cover and simmer for 20 minutes.
When cooked, the sauce should be smooth and creamy.

Remove from heat, mix the cornstarch with about
3 tablespoons cold water, then add to the sauce to
thicken. Season to taste with salt and pepper and,
if desired, add the garlic and the juice of the
remaining lime to taste. Pass the sauce through
a fine sieve and serve with the lobster pieces.

Pan-fried Mediterranean prawns and chicken breast

Serves 4
Prep: 20 minutes
Cook: 10 minutes

12 Mediterranean prawns
(if unavailable, substitute
jumbo shrimp)
----
1 lb 2 oz (500 g) chicken
breast
----
2 tablespoons peanut
(groundnut) oil
----
1 sprig chervil, chopped
----
1 clove garlic, finely
chopped

2 teaspoons finely chopped
fresh ginger
----
2 bird's-eye chiles*
(chillis), cut into fine
strips (if unavailable,
substitute piquin or
serrano chiles)
----
1 red bell pepper (red
pepper), diced
----
1 green bell pepper
(green pepper), diced

2 tablespoons balsamic
vinegar
----
juice of 1 lime
----
salt and black pepper
----
a pinch superfine (caster)
sugar
----
a few kaffir lime leaves,
snipped into thin strips
(if unavailable,
substitute basil leaves)

Shell and devein the prawns, removing the heads. Thinly
slice the chicken breast and the shelled prawns.

Heat the oil in a heavy-based saucepan. Add the chervil,
garlic, ginger, chiles and peppers. Fry gently over medium
heat for 2 minutes then add the balsamic vinegar.

Immediately add the chicken and the lime juice. Cook for
another minute, stirring constantly. Add the prawns. Season
to taste with salt and pepper and cook for 5 minutes more.

Remove from heat, add a pinch of sugar; mix gently. Serve
hot, over boiled sweet potatoes, if desired. Garnish with
the lime leaves.

Tuna layers with prawns and roasted mangoes

Serves 4
Prep: 20 minutes
Cook: 8 minutes
Bake: 5 minutes

1 lb 2 oz (500 g) tuna
fillets

----

8 Mediterranean prawns
(if unavailable,
substitute jumbo shrimp)

¼ bird's-eye chile*
(chilli) (if unavailable,
substitute piquin or
serrano chile)

¼ red bell pepper·
(red pepper)

----

6 basil leaves

----

1 tablespoon olive oil,
plus additional for
drizzling

----

2 cloves garlic, coarsely
chopped

----

salt and black pepper

----

1 tablespoon superfine
(caster) sugar

----

juice of 1 orange

----

2 mangoes, quartered
lengthwise and sliced

Shell and devein the prawns, removing the heads,
then finely chop the flesh. Thinly slice the
tuna fillets.

Purée the chile, pepper and basil leaves in a
blender or food processor. Heat the oil in a skillet
or frying pan, add the chile paste and cook for 2
minutes. Add the prawns and garlic; cook over high
heat for 2 minutes more. Season to taste with salt
and pepper.

Preheat oven to 400°F (200°C/gas 6), and grease and
flour a baking sheet. Arrange 4 slices of tuna on
the sheet and cover each slice with 1 tablespoon
of the prawn mixture. Cover with another slice of
tuna. Repeat several times, building up the layers.
Sprinkle lightly with salt. Bake for 5 minutes.

Caramelize the sugar in a saucepan then add the
orange juice and simmer for 2 minutes. Add the
mango slices to the saucepan and serve with the
tuna layers. Top all with a drizzle of olive oil.

Shark in a curry sauce with green tomatoes

Serves 4
Marinate: 12 hours
Prep: 15 minutes
Cook: 15 minutes

4 thick slices shark
(if unavailable, substitute
swordfish or white tuna)

----

1 tablespoon salt

----

3 cloves garlic, finely
chopped

----

1 teaspoon thyme flowers

----

3 limes

----

2 Scotch bonnet chiles*
(chillis)

----

salt and black pepper

----

2 tablespoons peanut
(groundnut) oil

----

1 onion, chopped

----

1 tablespoon finely chopped
scallion (spring onion)

----

1 tablespoon chopped
flat-leaf parsley leaves

----

1 tablespoon finely chopped
fresh ginger

----

1 small bunch cilantro
(coriander), chopped

----

4 green tomatoes,
finely diced

----

pinch ground cumin

----

3 tablespoons West Indian
Colombo powder*

The day before serving, remove and discard the skin
from the shark slices and place the slices in a
deep dish. Cover with cold water and add 1 tablespoon salt, 1 chopped clove garlic and ½ teaspoon
of the thyme flowers. Cut 1 of the limes into
quarters; squeeze the juice into the marinade; add
the lime pieces and 1 of the chiles, finely diced.
Add black pepper to taste and marinate in the
refrigerator for 12 hours.

The next day, heat the oil in a large, heavy-based
saucepan. Add the onion, scallion, parsley, the
remaining thyme flowers, the remaining chopped
garlic, the ginger and the cilantro, reserving
a few sprigs of cilantro for the garnish. Mix well
then add the green tomatoes. Sweat over low heat
for a few minutes to soften, stirring constantly
with a wooden spoon to prevent browning. Add the
cumin and black pepper to taste. Mix the Colombo
powder with a little water and add to the pot. Add
the juice of 1 of the limes and bring to a boil.

Drain the marinated shark pieces and add to the pot
with 2 small ladlefuls of the marinade, taking care
to avoid any pieces of chile. Stir and add water to
just cover the shark pieces. Season to taste with
salt and pepper. Add the remaining whole chile.
Simmer over low heat for 10 minutes.

When the shark pieces are cooked, remove the whole
chile, taking care that it does not burst. Stir in
the juice of the remaining lime.

Transfer the curry to a deep serving dish. Garnish
with a few fresh cilantro sprigs and serve with
Creole Rice (page 226).

Scallop and mirliton bake

Serves 4
Prep: 15 minutes
Cook: 25 minutes

3 green mirlitons*
(chayotes)
----
2 tablespoons olive oil
----
12 scallops
----
salt and black pepper
----
2 sprigs cilantro
(coriander), finely
chopped
----
1 sprig dill, finely
chopped
----
5 chives, finely chopped
----
1 sprig flat-leaf parsley,
finely chopped
----
1 shallot, finely chopped
----
1 clove garlic, finely
chopped

¼ Scotch bonnet chile*
(chilli), finely chopped
----
a grating fresh ginger

½ teaspoon saffron threads
----
juice of 1 lime
----
juice of 1 orange

Cut the mirlitons in half lengthwise and cook for
20 minutes in plenty of vigorously boiling water.
Using a teaspoon, carefully scoop out the flesh,
taking care not to break the skin. Set the skins
aside; chop the flesh into large dice.

Heat the oil in a skillet or frying pan and gently
fry the scallops on each side to sear. Season to
taste with salt and pepper. Add the cilantro, dill,
chives, parsley, shallots, garlic, chile and ginger;
cook for 20 minutes, stirring frequently. Stir in
the diced mirliton, the saffron and citrus juices.
Mix well and cook for 3 minutes on medium heat.

Remove the scallops and the mirliton pieces from
the sauce and place in the reserved mirliton skins.
Reduce the sauce to desired consistency and pour
over the stuffed mirlitons. Serve hot.

Conch ravioli with a crab and lemongrass sauce

Serves 4
Prep: 20 minutes
Cook: 10 minutes

2 tablespoons white-wine
vinegar
----
5 limes

2¼ lb (1 kg) young conch*
----
2 tablespoons peanut
(groundnut) oil
----
1 piece lemongrass, chopped
----
1 sprig cilantro (coriander)
----
1 sprig flat-leaf parsley,
chopped
----
1 clove garlic, chopped
----
salt and black pepper
----
pinch chili powder

3½ oz (100 g) baby spinach
leaves, chopped

½ lb (200 g) fresh pasta for
ravioli, cut into 3 in (8
cm) discs, or wonton skins
----
1 egg white
----
1 cup (250 ml/8 fl oz)
chicken stock

½ lb (200 g) crabmeat
----
1 tablespoon tomato purée
----
2 scallions (spring onions),
chopped

Add the white-wine vinegar and the juice of 3 limes to a basin of water. Wash the conchs in this water until the skin becomes rough to the touch. If they still slide under the fingers, repeat the procedure. Once the conchs are clean, beat the flesh to tenderize then chop finely. Mince in a blender or food processor. Set aside.

Heat the oil in a skillet or frying pan then gently fry half of the chopped lemongrass, cilantro, parsley and garlic. Add the minced conch; season to taste with salt and pepper. Add the chili powder and mix well. Bring to a simmer and cook for 1 to 2 minutes. Stir in the juice of 1 of the limes and the spinach and set aside to cool.

When the filling is cool, prepare the ravioli. Place a little of the filling in the middle of each pasta disc and fold into a half-moon shape. Brush the edges of the pasta with the egg white and seal, crimping the edges with a fork.

Meanwhile, bring the poultry stock to a boil in a saucepan with the broken-up crabmeat and the remaining lemongrass. Add the tomato purée. Season to taste with salt and pepper. When the mixture starts to boil, gently immerse the ravioli and cook over low heat for 5 minutes, stirring gently to prevent them sticking together.

Arrange the ravioli on a plate. Top with the sauce, the juice of the remaining lime and chopped scallions. Serve hot.

Creole seafood risotto

Serves 4
Stand: 8 to 24 hours
Prep: 20 minutes
Cook: 30 minutes

1 tablespoon olive oil
----
2 scallions (spring
onions), finely chopped
----
6 basil leaves, finely
chopped
----
3 cloves garlic, chopped
----
8 shallots, finely chopped

½ Scotch bonnet chile*
(chilli), finely chopped
----
14 oz (400 g) mixed
seafood such as cockles*,
clams, and squid, shelled
----
8 Mediterranean prawns
(if unavailable, substitute
jumbo shrimp)

½ teaspoon saffron threads
----
salt and black pepper
----
6 cups (1.5 litres/
2½ pints) fish stock
----
scant 1 cup (200 g/7 oz)
arborio rice
----
juice of 1 lime
----
2 tablespoons crème
fraîche (see page 62)
----
scant ½ cup (100 g/3½ oz)
grated Parmesan

The day before serving, make the crème fraîche
and let stand 8 to 24 hours or until very thick.
(The crème fraîche will keep, covered, in the
refriger-ator for up to 10 days.)

The next day, shell and devein the prawns, removing
the heads. Heat the oil in a deep-sided skillet or
frying pan. Gently fry the scallions, basil,
garlic, shallots and chile for 2 to 3 minutes. Mix
in the seafood and the prawns, then add the saffron.
Mix well. Season to taste with salt and pepper,
cover with the fish stock and cook for 2 minutes
more. Rinse the rice in cold water and then add.

Cook gently over very low heat for 20 minutes,
stirring occasionally using a wooden spoon, until
the rice has absorbed all the liquid. The rice
should be creamy. When cooked, remove from heat,
and add the lime juice and crème fraîche. Mix well
and serve hot, sprinkled with Parmesan.

Sauté of chatrou with tomatoes, sweet herbs and lime

Serves 6
Prep: 15 minutes
Cook: 40 minutes

4½ lb (2 kg) small
chatrou* (octopus)

----

3 tablespoons sunflower oil

----

3 limes

----

1 sprig thyme, finely
chopped

----

1 sprig flat-leaf parsley,
finely chopped

----

2 scallions (spring
onions), finely chopped

----

1 red onion, chopped

----

3 cloves garlic, chopped

----

4 large, very ripe
tomatoes, coarsely chopped

----

1 tablespoon tomato purée

----

1 Scotch bonnet chile*
(chilli)

----

salt and black pepper

Clean the chatrou; remove the ink sac and the suckers, and clean again. Squeeze the juice of 1 lime over the meat; chop finely and set aside.

Heat the oil in a heavy-based saucepan and gently sauté the chatrou pieces. Increase the heat to high for 2 to 3 minutes more, stirring constantly, then add the thyme, parsley, scallions, onion, two-thirds of the garlic, the tomatoes, the tomato purée and the whole chile. Season to taste with salt and pepper and cover with water.

Cover and cook over medium heat for 30 minutes. Reduce heat and add more water if necessary. Stew for 5 minutes more, until the sauce thickens. Remove from heat and add the juice of the remaining 2 limes and the remaining garlic.

Swordfish steaks stuffed with crab in a wasabi sauce

Serves 4
Marinate: 8 hours
Prep: 10 minutes
Cook: 5 minutes
Bake: 20 minutes

1 quantity Fish Marinade
(page 242)

---

4 swordfish steaks

---

2 tablespoons sunflower oil

---

1 clove garlic, finely
chopped

---

1 shallot, finely chopped

¼ bird's-eye chile*
(chilli), finely chopped
(if unavailable,
substitute piquin or
serrano chile)

---

1 sprig flat-leaf parsley,
finely chopped

½ lb (200 g) crabmeat

---

salt and black pepper

---

juice of 1 lime

---

3 tablespoons wasabi powder

---

1 teaspoon ground turmeric,
plus additional for
sprinkling

Wash the swordfish steaks and reserve 4 tablespoons of the marinade. Soak the swordfish steaks in the remaining marinade in the refrigerator overnight.

The next day, heat 1 tablespoon of the oil in a skillet or frying pan. Add the garlic, shallot, chile and parsley, reserving a little parsley for garnish. Fry gently over medium heat for 2 to 3 minutes. Add the crabmeat. Season to taste with salt and pepper and simmer for 3 to 4 minutes. Add the lime juice and remove from heat. Set aside.

Preheat oven to 400°F (200°C/gas 6). Drain the swordfish steaks and discard the marinade. Cut open the side of each steak, stuff with the crab mixture, then close and secure using a toothpick. Season with salt and pepper if desired. Grease and flour a baking dish. Place the stuffed steaks in the dish; bake for 20 minutes.

Place the wasabi, the 4 tablespoons of reserved marinade, the remaining 1 tablespoon oil and the turmeric in a blender or food processor. Season to taste with salt and pepper then purée and pass through a fine sieve. Serve the steaks with a drizzle of this sauce. Sprinkle with turmeric and garnish with chopped parsley.

Spaghetti with conch, prawns and vegetables

Serves 4
Prep: 20 minutes
Cook: 40 minutes

scant 1 cup (200 g/7 oz)
broccoli florets
----
scant ½ cup (100 g/3½ oz)
shelled fresh peas
----
7 oz (200 g) spaghetti
----
14 oz (400 g) conch*
(if unavailable,
substitute whelks)
----
3 tablespoons olive oil
----
2 scallions (spring
onions), finely chopped

2 cloves garlic, chopped
----
1 shallot, finely chopped
----
3 large tomatoes, diced

½ lb (200 g) shelled
Dublin Bay prawn tails
(if unavailable,
substitute jumbo shrimp)

¼ cup (50 g/2 oz) pitted
green olives, chopped
----
scant ½ cup (100 g/3½ oz)
diced green bell pepper
(green pepper)

1 bird's-eye chile*
(chilli), chopped
(if unavailable, substitute
piquin or serrano chile)
----
1 sprig thyme, chopped
----
1 teaspoon ground turmeric
----
salt and black pepper
----
1 sprig cilantro
(coriander),
finely chopped

Cook the broccoli florets in boiling water for 1 minute so that they remain crunchy. Cook the peas in a little butter for 2 minutes. Set vegetables aside.

Cook the spaghetti in plenty of boiling salted water until al dente. Drain and set aside. Cut the conch into thin slices and cook in a pressure cooker with 4 cups (1 litre/ 1¾ pint) of water for 20 minutes or simmer for at least 1 hour, or until cooked. Alternatively, cook the strips of conch in oil for 2 to 3 minutes, then blend for 2 seconds.

Heat the oil in a deep-sided skillet or frying pan and gently fry the scallions, garlic, shallot and tomatoes. Stew over low heat for 3 to 4 minutes more.

Add the conch, prawn tails, olives, finely diced green bell pepper, chile, thyme and turmeric. Season to taste with salt and pepper and mix well. Add the broccoli and peas at the last minute and serve hot, tossed with spaghetti and sprinkled with chopped cilantro.

Pan-fried spicy tuna tournedos with a z'habitant sauce

Serves 4
Marinate: 8 hours
Prep: 10 minutes
Cook: 15 minutes

1 quantity Fish Marinade
(page 242)

1¾ lb (800 g) tuna fillets

---

3 z'habitants* or large
Mediterranean prawns
(if unavailable,
substitute jumbo shrimp)

---

3 tablespoons sunflower oil

---

1 red onion, sliced into
rings

---

2 cloves garlic, finely
chopped

---

salt and black pepper

---

juice of 1 lime

---

a grating fresh ginger

---

3 scallions (spring onions)
or 9 chives, chopped

---

1 bird's-eye chile*
(chilli) (if unavailable,
substitute piquin or
serrano chile)

¼ cup (50 ml/2 fl oz)
white wine

Cut the tuna fillets into quarters then tie up
each piece with kitchen string to make tournedos.
Marinate in the refrigerator for 8 hours.
Meanwhile, shell and devein the z'habitants,
removing the heads.

Heat 1 tablespoon of the oil in a skillet or frying
pan and fry the onion rings until translucent;
set aside. Heat remaining oil and gently fry the
garlic. Brown the tournedos by cooking on each side
over low heat for 2 to 3 minutes, then remove from
the pan.

Increase the heat and place the z'habitants in the
pan. Season to taste with salt and pepper. Fry over
high heat for 5 minutes then add the lime juice, the
ginger, 1 of the chopped scallions and the chile.

Remove the z'habitant mixture from heat and purée
in a blender or food processor then return to pan.
Slowly stir in the white wine and simmer for 2
minutes. Pass through a fine sieve.

Arrange the tuna on a plate and top with the sauce.
Decorate with fried red onion rings and the
remaining chopped scallions.

Gnocchi with shark

Serves 4
Marinate: 8 hours
Prep: 10 minutes
Cook: 30 minutes

1 quantity Fish Marinade
(page 242)

1¾ lb (800 g) shark
fillets (if unavailable,
substitute swordfish or
white tuna)

----

2 tablespoons sunflower oil

----

1 sprig thyme, chopped

----

1 sprig flat-leaf parsley,
chopped

----

3 cloves garlic, chopped

----

1 onion, chopped

----

1 shallot, chopped

----

1 bay leaf

----

1 tablespoon red paste*

----

4 tomatoes

----

scant 1 cup (200 g/7 oz)
all-purpose (plain) flour

----

salt and black pepper

----

juice of 2 limes

Cut the shark fillets into large dice and marinate
in the refrigerator overnight.

The next day, heat the oil in a heavy-based
saucepan and gently fry the thyme, parsley, garlic,
onion and shallot. Add the bay leaf, red paste and
the tomatoes and cook over high heat for 5 to 10
minutes. Add the shark pieces and cover with water.
Cook for 10 minutes more.

Meanwhile, prepare the gnocchi. Season the flour
with salt and pepper to taste, then add enough
water to form a very firm dough. Make tiny
dumplings (about the same size as a whole almond)
by rolling pieces of the dough between your palms.
Remove the shark from the tomato mixture then add
the gnocchi. Add more salt and pepper if desired;
cook for 15 minutes.

When the gnocchi are cooked, add the shark again,
along with the lime juice. Serve hot.

Crab matatou

Serves 4
Marinate: 7 hours
Prep: 40 minutes
Cook: 20 minutes

1 quantity Fish Marinade
(page 242)
----
2 crabs
----
3 limes
----
3 slices smoked (streaky)
bacon
----
2 tablespoons peanut
(groundnut) oil
----
2 scallions (spring
onions), finely chopped

1 bunch flat-leaf parsley
----
1 shallot, finely chopped
----
1 sprig thyme, chopped
----
1 onion, finely chopped
----
2 tomatoes, finely chopped
----
salt and white pepper
----
1 teaspoon cumin
----
2 whole cloves

3 cloves garlic, chopped
----
2 Scotch bonnet chiles*
(chillis)
----
1 leaf bois d'Inde*
----
pinch curry powder
----
2 tablespoons olive oil

⅔ cup (150 g/5 oz) jasmine
rice, washed and drained
----
1 chive, chopped, plus
additional for garnish

Shell the crabs. Cut off the ends of the legs. Cut the crab flesh in half then half again. Break the pincers with the flat of a knife and marinate all the crab pieces in the refrigerator for 3 hours. Add the juice and zest of 1 of the limes to the marinade. Mix well and chill for 4 more hours.

Finely dice the bacon. Heat the peanut oil in a large saucepan and brown the scallion, chopped parsley, shallot, thyme, onion and tomatoes. Drain the crab pieces, retaining the marinade. Add the crab and the bacon to the saucepan. Sprinkle with white pepper, cumin, cloves and the garlic. Add a little salt, 1 of the chiles and the bois d'Inde. Stir well. Add 2 ladlefuls of the marinade and enough water to cover. Cook over low heat for 10 to 15 minutes. Add the curry powder and olive oil, then the rice. Mix well. Add the juice of the 2 remaining limes. Cook for 15 minutes more.

Arrange the crab in a serving dish with the rice and sauce. Garnish with the remaining whole chile, taking care not to burst it. Garnish the matatou* with the chopped chives and a few whole chives.

Creole paella

Serves 4
Prep: 20 minutes
Cook: 1 hour 30 minutes

4 chicken drumsticks

½ lb (200 g) chatrou*
(octopus)

----

14 oz (400 g) conch*

----

3 tablespoons sunflower oil

----

4 ouassous*, heads and
shells on, rinsed
(if unavailable,
substitute large crayfish)

½ lb (200 g) shelled
cockles*, rinsed (if
unavailable, substitute
hard-shell clams)

½ lb (200 g) mussels,
rinsed

----

1 bay leaf

----

salt and black pepper

----

1 tablespoon paella spices
(paprika, saffron, garlic,
and rosemary; prepared
versions are available)

----

1 Scotch bonnet chile*
(chilli), finely chopped

----

2 whole cloves

⅔ cup (150 g/5 oz) shelled
pigeon peas*

1 red bell pepper
(red pepper), diced

----

1 green bell pepper
(green pepper), diced

----

4 sprigs flat-leaf parsley

----

1 red onion, chopped

----

2 scallions (spring
onions), finely chopped

----

2 cloves garlic, chopped

----

1 cup (250 g/9 oz)
long-grain rice

----

juice of 2 limes

Cut the chicken drumsticks in half. Wash the chatrou and
pat dry; cut into small pieces. Wash the conch and pat dry;
beat with a meat mallet and cut into small pieces.

Heat the oil in a paella pan. Gently fry the chicken pieces
for 5 minutes, stirring frequently. Add the chatrou and
conch pieces and mix well. Cook for 10 to 15 minutes. Add
the ouassous, cockles, mussels and bay leaf; add enough
water to cover. Season with salt and black pepper. Add the
paella spices, chile and cloves.

Stir in the pigeon peas, the red and green bell peppers,
the parsley, onion, scallions and garlic. Cook for 30
minutes. Add the rice and more water if necessary to
cover; simmer for 40 minutes, until the water has been
absorbed. Remove from heat and add the lime juice. You
can add a little extra chile, to taste.

Macadam

Serves 4
Soak: 24 hours
Prep: 15 minutes
Cook: 10 minutes

2¼ lb (1 kg) salt cod

----

3 tablespoons olive oil

----

1 sprig thyme, finely chopped

----

2 sprigs flat-leaf parsley, finely chopped

----

2 cloves garlic, finely chopped

----

1 onion, finely chopped

----

scant 1 cup (200 g/7 oz) diced very ripe tomatoes, finely diced

----

1 bay leaf

¼ cup (50 g/2 oz) all-purpose (plain) flour

----

salt and black pepper

----

1 bird's-eye chile* (chilli), finely chopped (if unavailable, substitute piquin or serrano chile)

----

juice of 1 lime

----

1 quantity Creole rice (page 226)

The day before serving, place the salt cod in a large bowl of cool water to soak overnight. The next day, place the cod in a saucepan of water and boil vigorously over high heat. Drain the water and repeat several times. When the fish is completely rehydrated, drain and break it into pieces.

Heat the oil in a heavy-based saucepan and gently fry the thyme, parsley, garlic and onion. Add the tomatoes, the bay leaf and the flour. Season to taste with salt and pepper. Add the finely chopped chile. Simmer over medium heat for 2 to 3 minutes. Mix well.

Add the cod and simmer for 2 to 3 minutes more, stirring, then remove from heat and add the lime juice. Serve with Creole rice.

Martinique-style soaked cod

Serves 4
Soak: 24 hours
Prep: 10 minutes
Cook: 25 minutes

1 lb 2 oz (500 g) salt cod

----

7 oz (200 g) stale bread

----

3 tablespoons sunflower oil

----

3 scallions (spring
onions), finely chopped

----

3 sprigs flat-leaf
parsley, finely chopped

----

1 sprig thyme, finely
chopped

----

1 clove garlic, chopped

----

1 shallot, finely chopped

----

1 onion, finely chopped

----

1 Scotch bonnet chile*
(chilli), finely chopped

----

4 large, very ripe
tomatoes, finely diced

----

pinch ground cloves

----

salt and black pepper

----

juice of 1 lime

----

3 green bananas, finely
sliced under water

Place the salt cod in a large bowl of cool water to soak overnight.

The next day, place the cod in a saucepan of water and boil vigorously over high heat. Drain the water and repeat several times. When the fish is completely rehydrated, drain and break it into pieces.

Soak the stale bread in some water. Meanwhile, heat the oil in a heavy-based saucepan and gently fry the scallions, parsley, thyme, garlic, shallot, onion and chile. Add the finely diced tomatoes. Cook for 10 to 15 minutes. Add the cod, ground cloves and a little salt, if desired. Season with pepper to taste then cook for 10 minutes more. Remove from heat and add the lime juice.

Drain the soaked bread and squeeze out excess water. Break up with your fingers. Spread the bread on a plate or a banana leaf. Cover with a layer of banana slices then top with the cod mixture.

Meat and
Poultry

The Spices

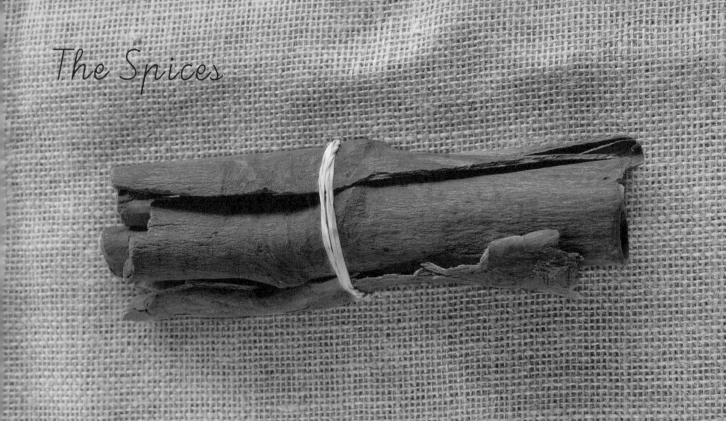

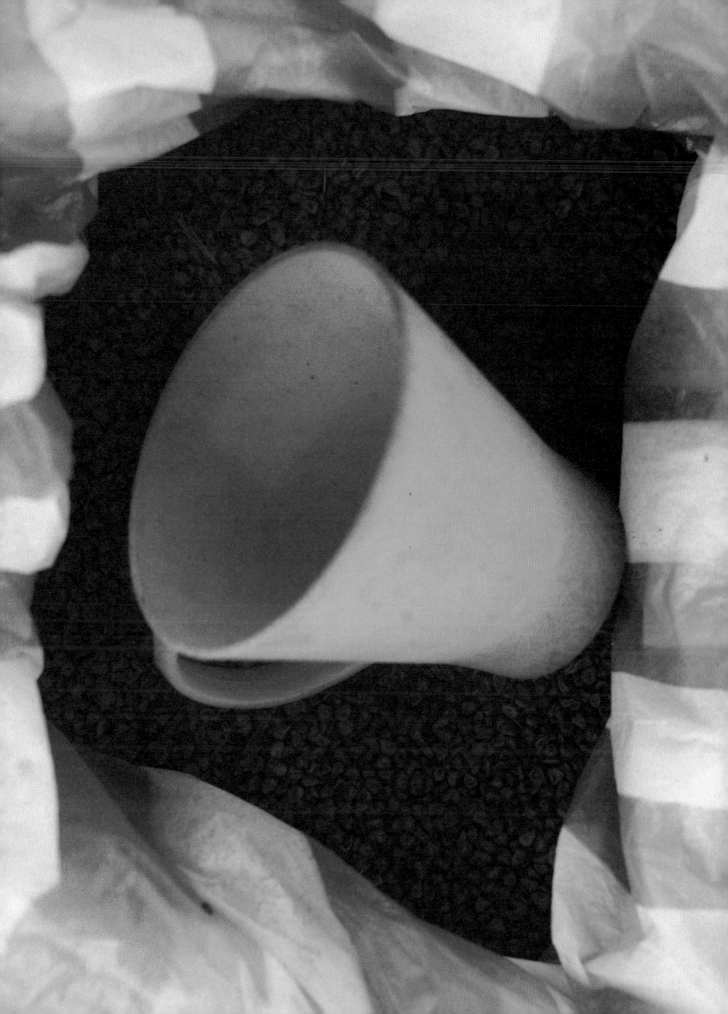

Spiced chicken snacks

Serves 4
Marinate: 48 hours
Prep: 20 minutes
Cook: 15 minutes

16 chicken drumsticks
----
1 sprig cilantro
(coriander)

¼ Scotch bonnet chile*
(chilli)
----
2 cloves garlic
----
juice of 6 limes
----
salt and black pepper
----
pinch quatre épices*
----
4 cups (1 litre/1¾ pint)
sunflower oil, for
deep-frying
----
1 quantity Traditional
'Sauce chien' (page 240)
----
1 quantity Ti'punch
(page 326)

Blend the cilantro, chile and garlic in a blender
or food processor and place in a large bowl with
the drumsticks and lime juice. Season to taste with
salt and pepper. Add the quatre épices and mix
well. Refrigerate for 48 hours.

Two days later, heat the oil in a large saucepan.
When very hot, add the drumsticks and cook for 10
to 15 minutes. When well browned, drain on paper
towels then serve with Traditional 'Sauce chien'
and accompany with Ti'punch.

Creole mini meat pies

Serves 4
Prep: 15 minutes
Cook: 6 minutes
Bake: 15 to 20 minutes

2 tablespoons sunflower oil
----
1 sprig flat-leaf parsley,
finely chopped
----
pinch chili powder
----
2 cloves garlic, finely
chopped
----
1 shallot, finely chopped
----
4 scallions (spring
onions), finely chopped
----
1 cup (250 g/9 oz) ground
(minced) beef
----
salt and black pepper
----
all-purpose (plain) flour,
for dusting
----
1 roll puff (flaky) pastry
----
1 egg, lightly beaten

Heat the oil in a heavy-based saucepan then gently fry the parsley, chili powder, garlic, shallot and scallions for 2 minutes. Add the ground beef, stirring vigorously to mix thoroughly. Season to taste with salt and pepper. Cook for 4 to 5 minutes more then remove from heat and set aside to cool.

Sprinkle the work surface with a little flour then spread out the puff pastry. Using a pastry cutter, cut out approximately 16 2¼-in (6-cm) circles.

Preheat oven to 350°F (180°C/gas 4). Place a tablespoonful of the cooled filling in the middle of half of the pastry discs, then cover with the remaining discs. Seal the edges well using a fork. Brush the egg over each pie. Bake for 15 to 20 minutes.

Chicken skewers with cumin

Serves 6
Marinate: 2 to 3 hours
Prep: 10 minutes
Grill or Bake: 10 minutes

1 quantity Meat and
Poultry Marinade
(page 242)

1¾ lb (800 g) chicken
breast
----
1 tablespoon sunflower oil
----
1 tablespoon cumin
----
1 clove garlic, chopped
----
1 sprig cilantro
(coriander), chopped
----
juice of 1 lime
----
salt and black pepper

Cut the chicken into large 1 in (2.5 cm) dice and
marinate in the refrigerator for 2 to 3 hours.

Drain the chicken pieces and thread onto skewers.
Cook the meat skewers on a barbecue or in a 350°F
(180°C/gas 4) oven for 10 minutes, turning so the
meat is well browned on all sides.

Place the oil, cumin, garlic and cilantro in a
large bowl. Add the lime juice and season to taste
with salt and pepper. Mix well and pour the sauce
over the meat skewers. Serve hot.

Grandmother's soup

Serves 6
Prep: 10 minutes
Cook: 1 hour 30 minutes

2¼ lb (1 kg) beef (brisket
and belly), cut into large
2 in (5 cm) pieces
----
1 clove garlic, chopped
----
2 turnips, chopped
----
2 carrots, chopped
----
1 potato, chopped
----
2 ribs (sticks) celery,
chopped
----
2 scallions (spring
onions), chopped
----
1 onion, peeled
----
4 whole cloves
----
2 beef bouillon (stock)
cubes, crumbled
----
salt and black pepper

Pour 4 quarts (4 litres/7 pints) water into a large
Dutch oven or stock pot. Bring to a boil and reduce
heat to simmer. Add the meat and cook for about
15 minutes, skimming any foam off the surface of
the water.

Place the garlic, turnips, carrots, potato, celery
and scallions in the pot. Stud the peeled onion
with the cloves and add to the pot, followed by
the bouillon cubes. Season to taste with salt
and pepper.

Cover and cook over low heat for 1 hour. Serve
very hot.

Calf's foot and vermicelli soup

Serves 4
Prep: 10 minutes
Cook: 30 minutes

2 calf's feet, cut into
generous 1-in (3-cm)
slices (ask your butcher
to do this for you)
----
2 carrots, quartered
----
2 turnips, quartered
----
1 onion
----
2 whole cloves
----
2 scallions
(spring onions)
----
1 sprig thyme, leaves
removed and chopped
----
1 sprig flat-leaf parsley
----
1 bay leaf
----
2 cloves garlic, crushed
----
2 chicken bouillon (stock)
cubes, crumbled
----
salt and black pepper
----
3 ribs (sticks) celery

¾ oz (20 g) vermicelli
pasta

Heat 8 cups (2 litres/3½ pints) water in a Dutch
oven or stock pot. When boiling, immerse the calf's
feet and cook, boiling vigorously, for 20 minutes.
Add the carrots and turnips. Stud the peeled onion
with the cloves and add to the pan along with the
scallions, thyme, parsley, bay leaf, garlic and
bouillon cubes. Season to taste with salt and
pepper. Cook for 10 minutes more. Add the celery
and the vermicelli and simmer for 3 to 4 minutes.
Adjust the seasoning if desired and serve hot.

Congo-style soup

Serves 4
Soak: 12 to 24 hours
Prep: 30 minutes
Cook: 45 minutes

4½ lb (2 kg) corned (salt) beef

1⅓ cups (300 g/11 oz) pigeon peas*

½ cup (100 g/3½ oz) coarsely chopped carrots

½ cup (100 g/3½ oz) coarsely chopped turnips

----

5 oz (150 g) cabbage, coarsely chopped

----

5 oz (150 g) eggplant (aubergine), chopped

½ cup (100 g/3½ oz) coarsely chopped giraumon*

1⅓ cups (300 g/11 oz) diced white yams*

1⅓ cups (300 g/11 oz) diced malangas*

1⅓ cups (300 g/11 oz) diced sweet potato

1⅓ cups (300 g/11 oz) diced ti'figues*

----

1 onion, finely chopped

2 cloves garlic, chopped

----

1 Scotch bonnet chile* (chilli)

----

1 bay leaf

----

2 cloves

----

salt and black pepper

----

3 tablespoons sunflower oil

----

4 very ripe tomatoes, finely diced

Cut the meat into small 1 in (2.5 cm) pieces and soak in a bowl of water overnight. The next day, cook the meat in a pressure cooker with 4 cups (1 litre/1¾ pint) water for 15 minutes. Alternatively, cook the meat in a saucepan with 8 cups (2 litres/3½ pint) water for 30 minutes. Then add the pigeon peas and continue cooking for 15 minutes.

Add the chopped and diced vegetables (except the tomatoes) to the pot and cover with water. Add the chile, bay leaf and cloves. Season to taste with salt and pepper and cook over medium heat for 30 minutes.

Heat the oil in a Dutch oven or stock pot. Add the tomatoes. Mix well and season to taste with salt and pepper. Pour the contents of the saucepan into the pan. Mix well and simmer for 3 minutes. Serve hot.

Salt pork blaff with West Indian vegetables

Serves 6
Prep: 15 minutes
Cook: 30 minutes

2¼ lb (1 kg)
salt pork

----

1 bouquet garni*

----

1 Scotch bonnet chile*
(chilli)

----

1 onion, coarsely chopped

----

3 cloves

----

1 plantain*

----

1 white yam*, chopped

----

1 whole stalk madère leaf*

----

3 carrots, quartered

¼ head cabbage, cut into
thirds

----

3 limes

----

1 sprig flat-leaf parsley

----

2 cloves garlic, chopped

----

3 scallions (spring
onions), finely chopped

----

pinch chili powder

----

black pepper

----

5 tablespoons peanut
(groundnut) oil

----

1 ripe banana

Cut the salt pork into 2 in (5 cm) pieces and place in a saucepan with enough water to cover. Add the bouquet garni, chile, onion, and cloves. Cover and boil for 15 minutes.

Peel the plantain and cut in half lengthwise; remove the ends and set aside. Peel the yam and chop into small pieces. Place the plantain and yam in a second saucepan with 4 cups (1 litre/1¾ pint) of salted water. Add the madère and the carrots. Add the cabbage and cook for 5 minutes more.

Drain the meat, retaining the stock, and place in a dish. Pour the juice of 1 of the limes over the meat. Transfer the cooked vegetables to the retained meat stock. Cover and cook for 5 minutes.

Remove a little of the cooking liquid and strain into a bowl. Add the chopped parsley, garlic, scallions, chili powder, black pepper and the juice of the remaining limes. Stir in the peanut oil. Pour this sauce over the meat. Serve the blaff* immediately, garnished with banana slices.

Ti'salé

Serves 6
Soak: 12 to 24 hours
Prep: 10 minutes
Cook: 2½ hours

3¼ lb (1.5 kg) corned
(salt) beef
----
3 tablespoons sunflower oil
----
3 cloves garlic, chopped
----
2 large onions, chopped
----
3 scallions (spring
onions), chopped
----
2 sprigs flat-leaf
parsley, chopped
----
2 sprigs thyme, chopped
----
2 bay leaves
----
2 cloves
----
2 cabbages, coarsely
chopped
----
juice of 4 limes
----
salt and black pepper

The day before serving, rehydrate the meat by placing it in a bowl full of water. The next day, transfer the meat to a saucepan containing 8 cups (2 litres/3½ pints) water; bring to a boil and cook for 1 hour 30 minutes. Drain meat, reserving cooking water.

Heat the oil in a heavy saucepan and gently fry 2 of the cloves of chopped garlic, the onions, scallions, parsley and thyme over low heat for 5 minutes. Add the drained meat, bay leaves, cloves and half the cooking water. Cook for 40 minutes. Stir in the cabbages and add more water if necessary. Cook for about 10 minutes more - the cabbage should still be crunchy.

When cooked, add the lime juice and the remaining chopped clove of garlic. Season to taste with salt and pepper.

The name of this dish comes from the French phrase, 'petit salé' which means, 'bits of salted meat'

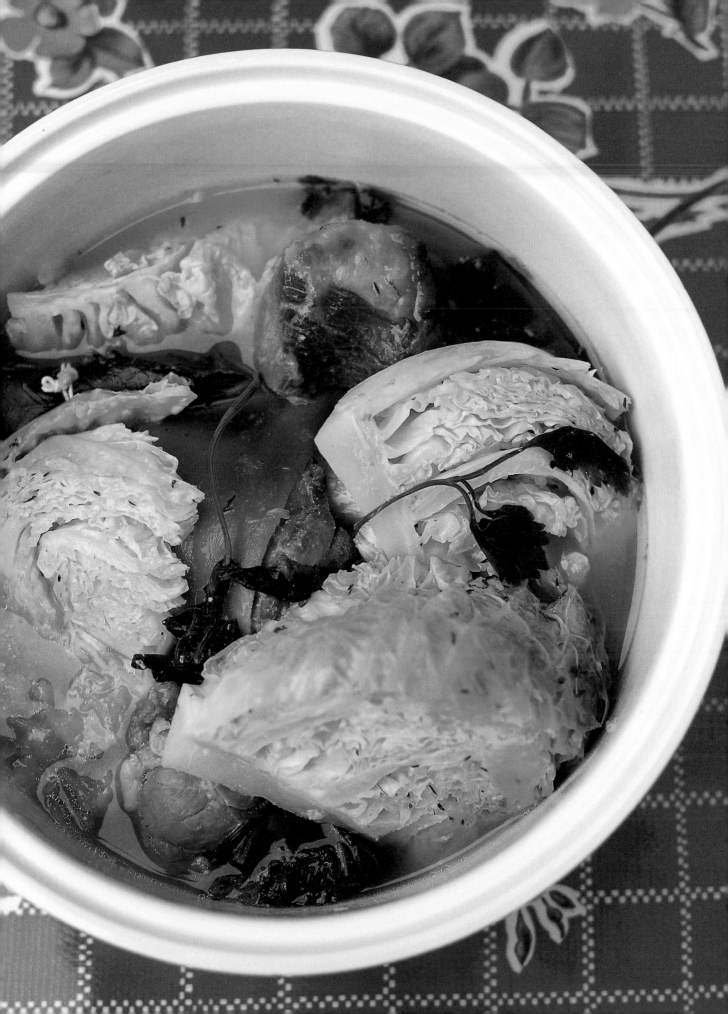

Colombo pork loin curry

Serves 6
Marinate: 2 to 3 hours
Prep: 15 minutes
Cook: 1 hour

1 quantity Meat and
Poultry Marinade
(page 242)

2¼ lb (1 kg) pork loin
with rind
----
3 tablespoons sunflower oil
----
2 tablespoons chicken
bouillon granules (powdered
poultry stock or 1 chicken
stock cube, crumbled)
----
1 onion, chopped

2 cloves garlic, chopped
----
1 sprig thyme, leaves
removed and chopped
----
1 sprig flat-leaf parsley
----
1 bay leaf
----
2 cloves
----
1 whole chile (chilli)
----
scant ½ cup (100 g/3½ oz)
West Indian Colombo powder*

1 eggplant (aubergine),
peeled and diced
----
2 potatoes, peeled and
diced
----
3 zucchini (courgettes),
sliced
----
1 tablespoon cornstarch
(cornflour)
----
juice of 2 limes
----
salt and black pepper

Cut the pork loin into large chunks and marinate in the
refrigerator for 2 to 3 hours.

Heat 2 tablespoons of the oil in a heavy-based saucepan.
When hot, add the drained meat pieces. Sear them over high
heat for 10 minutes without letting them brown.

Dissolve the bouillon in 4 cups (1 litre/1¾ pint) of water
and pour into the saucepan over the pork. Stir in the
onion, garlic, thyme, parsley, bay leaf, cloves, whole
chile and the Colombo powder mixed with a little water.
Cover and cook at a vigorous boil for 15 minutes.

Add the eggplant, potatoes and zucchini; simmer, covered,
for 25 minutes. When the meat is cooked, remove it from the
sauce and keep hot.

Strain the sauce into a fresh pan, removing the herbs.
Cook on medium heat; add the corn-starch, mixed with a
little water, and stir it into the sauce to thicken it.
Add the lime juice and the remaining oil. Top the meat
with the sauce. Serve immediately.

Guiana-style haunch of wild boar

Serves 6
Marinate: 48 hours
Prep: 10 minutes
Roast: 40 minutes

1 haunch pac*

----

2 shallots, chopped

----

4 cloves garlic, chopped,
plus additional cloves,
crushed, to stud the roast

----

2 sprigs flat-leaf
parsley, chopped

----

1 sprig thyme, leaves
removed and chopped

----

1 bay leaf

----

1 onion, chopped

----

2 scallions (spring
onions), chopped

----

2 cups (500 ml/18 fl oz)
white wine

----

salt and black pepper

----

3 tablespoons sunflower oil

----

5 tablespoons ground cumin

----

6 bois d'Inde* seeds

----

2 cloves

----

3 tablespoons white-wine
vinegar

----

1 tablespoon superfine
(caster) sugar

Two days before serving, remove the rind from the
pac, along with any tendons. Pierce the meat with
plenty of crushed garlic cloves (how many you add
is according to your taste).

Place it in a large dish then add the shallots,
the 4 cloves garlic, the parsley, thyme, bay leaf,
onion, scallions and wine. Season to taste with
salt and pepper. Refrigerate for 24 hours then turn
the meat over so that the whole haunch is marinated.
Refrigerate for another 24 hours.

The next day, preheat oven to 350°F (180°C/gas 4).
Drain the meat, retaining the marinade, and place
in a baking tray. Pour the oil over the meat and
roast for 40 minutes, basting frequently with the
reserved marinade. At the end of cooking, add the
cumin, the bois d'Inde seeds and the cloves.

Place the roast on a serving plate. Deglaze the
baking dish with the vinegar and a little of the
marinade. Add the sugar and pass through a sieve.
Serve the meat with this sauce.

Babette's West Indian-style pork ragout

Serves 8
Marinate: 2 to 3 hours
Prep: 15 minutes
Cook: 50 minutes

4½ lb (2 kg) pork loin
with rind

----

1 quantity Meat and Poultry
Marinade (page 242)

----

2 tablespoons sunflower oil

----

1 tablespoon superfine
(caster) sugar

----

2 bay leaves

----

2 scallions (spring
onions)

----

1 sprig thyme, leaves
removed and finely chopped

----

1 chive

----

1 onion, coarsely chopped

----

clove/s garlic, coarsely
chopped

----

pinch ground cumin

----

pinch quatre épices*

----

salt and black pepper

----

2 tablespoons chicken
bouillon granules
(powdered poultry stock,
or two chicken stock
cubes, crumbled)

----

2 tablespoons cornstarch
(cornflour)

Cut the pork loin into large pieces and marinate
in the refrigerator for 2 to 3 hours.

Heat the oil with the sugar in a deep-sided skillet
or frying pan to caramelize it. When the caramel is
very brown, almost black, add the drained pieces of
meat and mix immediately. Brown the meat well for
about 10 minutes, occasionally adding a few drops
of water.

When the meat is well caramelized, add enough water
to cover. Add the bay leaves, scallions, thyme,
chives, onion and garlic, to taste, then the cumin
and quatre épices. Season to taste with salt and
pepper. Cover and boil vigorously over medium heat
for 40 minutes.

When the meat is cooked, remove from the liquid and
keep warm. Strain the cooking liquid into a saucepan and return to the stove. Mix the cornstarch and
bouillon into 1 cup (250 ml/8 fl oz) water and pour
into the cooking liquid. Reduce and thicken for
about 3 minutes then pour over the meat. Serve hot.

Pork cheek stew browned with Caribbean spices

Serves 4
Marinate: 8 hours
Prep: 10 minutes
Cook: 55 minutes

2¼ lb (1 kg) pork cheek,
cut into chunks
----
2 tablespoons sunflower oil
----
1 teaspoon superfine
(caster) sugar
----
2 tablespoons arôme
patrelle*
----
1 sprig flat-leaf parsley,
chopped
----
2 onions, chopped

4 scallions (spring
onions), chopped
----
2 shallots, chopped
----
1 clove garlic, chopped
----
a grating fresh ginger
----
1 sprig thyme, leaves
removed and chopped
----
2 cloves

½ tablespoon quatre épices*

2 bay leaves
----
1 small piece Scotch
bonnet chile* (chilli)
----
1 tablespoon chicken
bouillon granules
(powdered poultry stock or
one chicken stock cube,
crumbled)
----
1 teaspoon cornstarch
(cornflour)

Place the pork in a bowl. Add the marinade ingredients then
knead them into the meat with your hands. Marinate in the
refrigerator for about 8 hours.

Heat the oil and sugar in a heavy-based saucepan. When the
sugar has caramelized, add the meat then the arôme patrelle.
Cook gently for 5 minutes until the pork is well browned on
all sides.

Mix in the parsley, onions, scallions, shallots and garlic.
Add the ginger, thyme, cloves and quatre épices. Season to
taste with salt and pepper.

Marinade

2 cloves garlic, chopped
----
pinch ground cumin
----
1 tablespoon white-wine
vinegar
----
2 tablespoons sunflower oil

Continue to brown the meat over high heat for 10 minutes,
stirring constantly and occasionally adding a few drops of
water. At the end of the 10 minutes, add enough water to
cover the meat. Add the bay leaves and the small piece of
chile. Dissolve the bouillon in a little water and pour
into the saucepan. Simmer over low heat for 40 minutes.

If desired, thicken the sauce by mixing the corn-starch
with 3 tablespoons of water and adding this mixture to the
pan. Serve hot.

Christmas ham with pineapple

Serves 6
Soak: 4 to 12 hours
Prep: 10 minutes
Cook: 2 hours 10 minutes

1 lightly salted
bone-in ham

----

1 sprig thyme

----

2 sprigs flat-leaf parsley

----

4 bay leaves

----

5 cloves

----

1 Scotch bonnet chile*
(chilli)

----

1 pineapple

----

3 tablespoons cane sugar
or white (caster) sugar

----

2 tablespoons sunflower oil

Clean and scrape the skin of the ham then soak overnight in a large container of water.

The next day, drain off the water. Place the ham in a saucepan with 6 quarts (6 litres/10½ pints) water and the thyme, parsley, bay leaves, cloves and the whole chile, then bring to a boil and cook for 2 hours. Test the ham with a skewer from time to time (the juices will run clear when it is cooked). When it is ready, drain and set aside.

Peel the pineapple and cut it into not-too-thick slices. Put the slices in a saucepan with 1 tablespoon of the sugar and brown them.

Place the ham in a baking dish and sprinkle with the remaining 2 tablespoons sugar and the oil; place under the broiler (grill) to caramelize. When caramelized, serve with the pineapple slices.

Breadfruit hot pot with Colombo curry

Serves 6
Prep: 15 minutes
Cook: 1 hour 15 minutes

3 tablespoons sunflower oil

----

1 onion, chopped

----

2 cloves garlic, chopped

----

4 scallions (spring
onions), finely chopped

----

2 bay leaves, finely
chopped

----

1 sprig flat-leaf parsley,
finely chopped

----

1 sprig thyme, finely
chopped

----

3 lightly salted pig tails,
cut into small pieces

½ lb (200 g) smoked
(streaky) bacon, finely
diced

----

3 large, very ripe tomatoes

----

1 breadfruit (about 2¼ lb/
1 kg), peeled and diced
(available frozen from
specialty stores and online)

¼ cup (50 g/2 oz) West
Indian Colombo powder*

----

salt and black pepper

----

juice of 1 lime

----

1 Scotch bonnet chile*
(chilli), finely chopped

Heat the oil in a heavy-based saucepan and gently
fry the onions, garlic, scallions, bay leaves,
parsley and thyme, without browning them. Add the
pieces of pig tail, the bacon and the tomatoes.
Mix well and simmer for 3 to 4 minutes, taking
care that nothing sticks to the bottom of the pan.

Pour in 4 cups (1 litre/1¾ pints) of water, bring
to a boil and cook over medium heat for 30 minutes.
Add the breadfruit and the Colombo powder. Season
to taste with salt and pepper then cook over medium
heat for about 40 minutes, until the mixture
becomes smooth. Mix in the lime juice. Serve hot.
Add the chile to taste.

West Indian cassoulet

Serves 6
Soak: 24 hours
Prep: 15 minutes
Cook: 1 hour 10 minutes

14 oz (400 g) salt beef
----
14 oz (400 g) pork shoulder
----
3 tablespoons sunflower oil
----
6 cups (1.5 kg/3¼ lb)
pigeon peas,* shelled

½ lb (200 g) bacon
(streaky bacon), chopped
----
5 oz (150 g) lardons*
----
2 scallions (spring onions)
----
3 tablespoons tomato purée

3½ oz (100 g) West Indian
andouillette (tripe*
sausage)
----
2 smoked chicken
drumsticks, cut in half
----
1 pinch cayenne pepper
----
juice of 1 lemon

The day before serving, soak the beef and the pork
in plenty of water. The next day, cut the soaked
meats into small pieces.

Heat the oil in a heavy-based saucepan, gently
fry the pigeon peas for 10 minutes then cover
with water. Add the beef, pork, bacon, lardons,
scallions, tomato purée and andouillette, then
simmer for 1 hour, stirring occasionally. Season
with additional salt if desired.

Four minutes before the end of the cooking time,
add the chicken, the chile, to taste, and the lemon
juice. Serve hot.

Browned beef stew with vegetables

Serves 4
Marinate: 2 to 3 hours
Prep: 10 minutes
Cook: 55 minutes

1 quantity Meat and
Poultry Marinade (page
242)

2¼ lb (1 kg) rump steak
----
3 tablespoons sunflower oil
----
1 tablespoon superfine
(caster) sugar
----
2 bay leaves
----
1 sprig thyme, chopped
----
1 sprig flat-leaf parsley,
chopped
----
2 scallions (spring
onions), chopped
----
2 cloves
----
2 onions, chopped
----
2 cloves garlic, chopped
----
1 Scotch bonnet chile*
(chilli)
----
2 carrots, cut into sticks
----
2 potatoes, chopped
----
2 turnips, cut into sticks
----
1 tablespoon lemon vinegar

Chop the meat into large dice and marinate in
the refrigerator for 2 to 3 hours. Drain and
reserve marinade.

Heat the oil and the sugar in deep-sided skillet
or frying pan. Let the sugar caramelize. When very
brown, stir in the pieces of meat, then continue
stirring over high heat until there is no more
liquid. Brown the meat well, occasionally adding
a few drops of water.

Add enough water to cover the meat. Fish out the
onion and garlic from the marinade and add to the
pan. Add the bay leaves, thyme, parsley, scallions,
cloves, and the chopped 2 onions and 2 cloves
of garlic. Add the whole chile, taking care that
it does not break. Stew over medium heat for
30 minutes.

Add the carrots, potatoes, turnips and vinegar,
then cover and cook for 15 minutes more. Serve hot.

If lemon vinegar is not available locally, you can
make your own. Heat 1 small bottle white-wine
vinegar (8 fl oz/250 ml) in a stainless-steel pan.
Cut the zest from 1 large lemon in a continuous
strip into a bowl and add the warmed vinegar. Let
it cool so that it infuses, strain the mixture and
then bottle it and keep it in a cool dark place.

Guadeloupe-style pan-fried entrecote steaks

Serves 2
Stand: 6 to 8 hours
Prep: 5 minutes
Cook: 5 minutes

4 large beef rib steaks
----
salt and black pepper
----
2 cloves garlic, finely chopped
----
2 tablespoons sunflower oil
----
2 tablespoons white-wine vinegar
----
1 onion, finely chopped
----
1 scallion (spring onion), finely chopped

Place the rib steaks in a large bowl. Season with salt and pepper and add half the chopped garlic. Mix well so that the seasoning penetrates the meat. Let stand in the refrigerator for 6 to 8 hours.

Heat the oil in a skillet or frying pan and brown the steaks on both sides. Place them on a serving plate. Deglaze the pan with the vinegar. Stir in the onion, scallion and remaining chopped garlic, then cook gently for 1 to 2 minutes, stirring constantly. Top the steaks with this slightly thickened sauce. Serve hot.

Veal chops with sweet spices

Serves 4
Stand: 24 hours
Prep: 10 minutes
Cook: 8 minutes

4 veal chops
----
5 tablespoons sunflower oil
----
salt and black pepper
----
2 sprigs thyme, leaves
removed and chopped
----
3 cloves garlic
----
2 shallots
----
2 sprigs flat-leaf parsley
----
juice of 1 lemon

Soak the veal chops in 3 tablespoons of the oil
seasoned with salt and pepper. Let stand in the
refrigerator overnight.

The next day, heat the remaining 2 tablespoons of
oil in a skillet or frying pan. When hot, brown the
meat for 2 minutes on each side.

Chop the thyme, garlic and shallots in a blender
or food processor then add to the pan and mix well.
Sprinkle the meat with a few drops of water. Turn
the chops over. Continue cooking for another
3 minutes on each side.

Place the meat on serving plates and top with the
chopped parsley and the lemon juice. If desired,
garnish with caramelized onion rings.

Lamb in a turmeric and wasabi white sauce with pistachios

Serves 4
Stand: 8 to 24 hours
Prep: 10 minutes
Cook: 50 minutes

2 tablespoons sunflower oil

2¼ lb (1 kg) lamb
stew meat
----
1 large onion, cut into
large pieces
----
3 cloves garlic, sliced

¼ chile (chilli), chopped
----
1 sprig thyme, leaves
removed and chopped
----
1 bay leaf
----
salt and black pepper
----
2 to 3 tablespoons (30 g/
1 oz) butter
----
2 tablespoons all-purpose
(plain) flour
----
1 egg yolk
----
2 tablespoons crème
fraîche (see page 62)
----
pinch ground turmeric
----
3 tablespoons wasabi powder
----
juice of 2 lemons
----
2 oz (50 g) pistachio nuts,
shelled

The day before serving, make the crème fraîche
and let stand 8 to 24 hours or until very thick.
(The crème fraîche will keep, covered, in the
refrigerator for up to 10 days.)

The next day, heat the oil in a heavy-based saucepan, then add the lamb. Cook without browning to
sear the meat. Add the onion, garlic and chile to
the saucepan. Add the thyme and the bay leaf.
Season to taste with salt and pepper. Cover and
cook for 45 minutes. Remove from heat.

Melt the butter in a small saucepan then add the
flour. Add the cooking juices from the meat. Simmer
for a few minutes more, then remove from heat. Mix
the egg yolk, crème fraîche, turmeric and wasabi
powder and add this mixture, along with the lemon
juice, to the sauce.

Place the lamb on a serving plate and top with the
sauce. Sprinkle with the pistachios.

Spicy lamb skewers

Serves 4
Stand: 24 hours
Prep: 10 minutes
Cook: 5 to 6 minutes

1¾ lb (800 g) boneless
leg of lamb, cut into
large chunks
----
2 tablespoons sunflower oil
----
pinch ground cumin
----
pinch ground cardamom
----
3 cloves garlic, finely
chopped
----
salt and black pepper

The day before serving, place the meat in a large
bowl. Add the oil, cumin, cardamom and garlic.
Season with salt and pepper. Mix well; let stand
in the refrigerator for 24 hours.

The next day, drain the meat pieces and thread onto
skewers. Barbecue, preferably over wood charcoal,
for 5 to 6 minutes, turning so the meat is well
browned on all sides.

Serve hot. If desired, serve with grilled vegetables on a bed of fresh green salad leaves dressed
with plenty of vinegar.

Pan-fried chicken breast with cinnamon and coconut milk

Serves 4
Prep: 20 minutes
Cook: 25 minutes
Bake: 5 minutes

2 coconuts

----

2 tablespoons sunflower oil

1¾ lb (800 g) chicken
breast

----

salt and black pepper

----

1 sprig flat-leaf parsley,
chopped

----

pinch chopped cilantro
(coriander)

----

2 whole cloves

----

2 onions, chopped

----

2 cloves garlic, chopped

----

pinch ground cinnamon

----

2 to 3 tablespoons (30 g/
1 oz) butter

----

2 to 3 tablespoons all-
purpose (plain) flour

----

1 cup (250 ml/8 fl oz)
coconut milk

Break open the coconuts and finely grate the flesh;
set aside.

Heat the oil in a heavy-based saucepan over low
heat and brown the chicken breast. Season to taste
with salt and pepper. Add the grated coconut,
parsley, cilantro, cloves, onions and garlic.
Pour in 1 cup (250 ml/8 fl oz) water. Simmer for
3 minutes.

Preheat oven to 400°F (200°C/gas 6). Remove the
chicken breast and arrange on a plate. Sprinkle
with the cinnamon.

Pass the sauce through a fine-mesh sieve. Make a
thickening paste by melting the butter and stirring
in the flour; let it cool, then stir it into the
sieved sauce, whisking vigorously. Stir in the
coconut milk. Adjust the seasoning if desired.

Top the chicken with this creamy sauce. Bake for
5 minutes. Serve immediately. If desired, serve
with snow peas and red bell pepper sautéd in butter.

Colombo curry

Serves 4
Marinate: 2 to 3 hours
Prep: 15 minutes
Cook: 55 minutes

1 quantity Meat and
Poultry Marinade
(page 242)
----
4 chicken drumsticks
----
4 tablespoons sunflower oil
----
salt and black pepper
----
1 sprig thyme, chopped
----
1 sprig flat-leaf parsley,
coarsely chopped
----
2 onions, coarsely chopped

2 cloves garlic, chopped
----
1 eggplant (aubergine),
chopped
----
1 red bell pepper (red
pepper), chopped
----
2 green bell peppers
(green peppers), chopped
----
1 zucchini (courgette)
----
scant ½ cup (100 g/3½ oz)
West Indian Colombo powder*

2 tablespoons chicken
bouillon granules
(powdered poultry stock or
1 chicken stock cube,
crumbled)
----
2 bay leaves
----
1 Scotch bonnet chile*
(chilli)

½ teaspoon quatre épices*
----
juice of 2 limes

Bone the chicken. Marinate the meat in the refrigerator for
2 to 3 hours, then drain.

Heat the oil in a heavy-based saucepan over high heat and
cook the chicken for 2 to 3 minutes to sear without
browning. Season to taste with salt and pepper. Add 4 cups
(1 litre/1¾ pints) water and stir in the chopped herbs,
onions, garlic and vegetables. Mix well.

Mix the Colombo powder with a little water then stir in the
bouillon granules. Pour the bouillon mixture into the
saucepan. Add the bay leaves, the whole chile, taking care
that it does not burst, and the quatre épices, then cook
over medium heat for 40 minutes more.

Remove the chicken from the saucepan but keep the sauce
over the heat. Adjust the seasoning if desired. Pass the
sauce through a sieve and return to the heat. Add the lime
juice and allow the sauce to thicken.

Serve the chicken topped with the sauce and garnish with
fine slices of red and green bell pepper.

Buccaneer chicken drumsticks with 'Sauce chien'

Serves 4
Marinate: 24 hours
Prep: 15 minutes
Cook: 30 minutes

4 chicken drumsticks
----
1 sprig flat-leaf parsley
----
1 onion
----
2 scallions (spring onions)
----
3 cloves garlic

¼ Scotch bonnet chile*
(chilli)
----
salt and black pepper
----
juice of 3 limes
----
2 tablespoons sunflower oil
----
1 quantity Traditional
'Sauce chien' (page 240)

The day before serving, place the chicken drumsticks in a large container. Season with salt and pepper. Blend the parsley, onion, scallions, garlic and chile in a blender or food processor. Add the blended mixture, the lime juice and 1 tablespoon of the oil to the chicken; mix well and marinate in the refrigerator for 24 hours.

Drain the chicken drumsticks, retaining the marinade. Heat the remaining oil in a heavy-based saucepan. When hot, sear the drum-sticks, stirring constantly. Add the marinade then cover and cook over medium heat for 8 to 10 minutes.

Remove the chicken from the saucepan and grill for 10 minutes over wood charcoal, sprinkling occasion-ally with a few drops of water until the chicken is perfectly cooked. Serve the drumsticks topped with Traditional 'Sauce chien'

Fricassee of caramelized chicken

Serves 4
Marinate: 24 hours
Prep: 30 minutes
Cook: 50 minutes

1 free-range chicken
----
salt and black pepper
----
2 tablespoons white-wine
vinegar
----
5 cups (1.25 litres/
2 pints) sunflower oil
----
6 cloves garlic, chopped
----
3 sweet potatoes, diced
----
1 teaspoon arôme patrelle*

1 teaspoon graines à
roussir*
----
1 scallion (spring onion),
finely sliced
----
2 onions, chopped
----
1 shallot, chopped
----
1 bay leaf
----
1 sprig thyme, chopped
----
1 whole chile (chilli)

a grating fresh ginger
----
2 whole cloves
----
1 tablespoon chicken
bouillon granules
(powdered poultry stock or
one chicken stock cube
crumbled)
----
1 tablespoon cornstarch
(cornflour)

The day before serving, cut the chicken into 8 pieces and
place in a large bowl. Season. Add the white-wine vinegar,
1 tablespoon of the oil and one-third of the chopped
garlic. Marinate for 24 hours.

The next day, heat 3 tablespoons of the oil in a heavy-
based saucepan. Drain the chicken pieces, retaining the
marinade, then sear them in the very hot oil. Continue to
fry the meat, adding the arôme patrelle to color it. Season
with the graines à roussir and salt and pepper. Add the
scallions and a little water.

Add the onions, shallot and remaining garlic, the bay leaf,
thyme and chile. Cover with water and cook over medium heat
for 15 to 20 minutes. Add the ginger and cloves. Dissolve
the bouillon in a little water. Add the cornstarch, pour
the mixture over the chicken and simmer for 10 minutes.

Immerse the sweet potatoes in boiling salted water and cook
for 15 minutes. Heat the remaining oil until very hot.
Drain the sweet potatoes, immerse them in the oil and cook
for 2 to 3 minutes. Serve the fricassee over the sweet
potatoes, garnished with tomato and parsley.

Chicken stew with ginger

Serves 4
Marinate: 2 to 3 hours
Prep: 15 minutes
Cook: 35 minutes

1 quantity Meat and Poultry
Marinade (page 242)
----
1 chicken
----
2 tablespoons sunflower oil
----
1 tablespoon white
(granulated) sugar
----
1 scallion (spring onion)
----
1 sprig thyme
----
1 sprig flat-leaf parsley
----
2 cloves garlic, chopped
----
2 whole cloves
----
2 teaspoons grated fresh
ginger
----
1 red onion, sliced
----
pinch ground cumin
----
pinch quatre épices*
----
salt and black pepper
----
1 Scotch bonnet chile*
(chilli)
----
1 tablespoon chicken
bouillon granules
(powdered poultry stock or
1 chicken stock cube,
crumbled)

Cut the chicken into 8 pieces and marinate in the refrigerator for 2 to 3 hours.

Heat the oil and sugar in a heavy-based saucepan. When the sugar caramelizes, add the drained chicken pieces and brown them well, adding a few drops of water from time to time.

Add the whole scallion, thyme sprig and parsley sprig to the saucepan, as well as the garlic, cloves, ginger and onion. Sprinkle with the cumin and quatre épices.

Add enough water to cover the chicken. Season to taste with salt and pepper. Add the whole chile, without letting it burst, and cook over medium heat for 30 minutes more.

At the end of the cooking time, add the bouillon dissolved in a little water, simmer for 2 to 3 minutes, then remove the chicken pieces from the sauce. Pass the sauce through a sieve. Place the chicken pieces on a serving plate and top with the sauce. Serve hot.

Chicken drumsticks with bélangère in a Colombo curry sauce

Serves 4
Marinate: 2 to 3 hours
Prep: 10 minutes
Cook: 30 minutes

1 quantity Meat and Poultry
Marinade (page 242)
----
4 chicken drumsticks
----
2 tablespoons peanut
(groundnut) oil
----
1 sprig flat-leaf parsley,
coarsely chopped
----
2 cloves garlic, coarsely
chopped
----
a grating fresh ginger
----
2 shallots, coarsely
chopped
----
1 bélangère*, sliced
----
salt and black pepper
----
3 sprigs thyme
----
pinch ground cardamom
----
1 bay leaf
----
3 oz (80 g) West Indian
Colombo powder*
----
pinch ground cinnamon
----
2 tablespoons cornstarch
(cornflour)

Marinate the chicken drumsticks in the refrigerator
for 2 to 3 hours.

Heat the oil in a heavy-based saucepan. When very
hot, add the drained chicken. Mix immediately, then
add the parsley, garlic, ginger, shallots and the
bélangère. Season to taste with salt and pepper.
Simmer over medium heat for 5 minutes then add
enough water to cover.

Add the thyme, cardamom, bay leaf, Colombo powder
and cinnamon. Cover and cook over medium heat for
20 minutes. Remove the chicken from the sauce and
set aside.

Pass the sauce through a sieve then return to the
saucepan and thicken by adding the cornstarch.
Serve hot, garnished with the thyme sprigs.

Saddle of rabbit in cocoa mustard

Serves 4
Stand: 8 to 24 hours
Prep: 15 minutes
Cook: 50 minutes

1 tablespoon unsweetened cocoa powder

5 tablespoons mustard

2 tablespoons crème fraîche (see page 62)

3 tablespoons peanut (groundnut) oil

1 rabbit (about 3¼ lb/1.5 kg), cut into small pieces

1 sprig thyme, chopped

1 sprig flat-leaf parsley

1 sprig tarragon, chopped

2 cloves garlic, chopped

2 shallots, chopped

4 chives, chopped

2 bay leaves

2 tablespoons chicken bouillon granules (powdered poultry stock or two chicken stock cubes, crumbled)

salt and black pepper

½ green bell pepper (green pepper), cut into strips

½ red bell pepper (red pepper), cut into strips

2 tablespoons (25 g/1 oz) butter, melted

2 teaspoons white (caster) sugar

The day before serving, make the crème fraîche and let stand 8 to 24 hours or until very thick. (The crème fraîche will keep, covered, in the refrigerator for up to 10 days.)

The next day, mix the cocoa with the mustard, add the crème fraîche and set aside. Heat the oil in a heavy-based saucepan. When very hot, fry the rabbit for 2 to 3 minutes, stirring well. Add the thyme, parsley, tarragon, garlic, shallots, chives and the bay leaf, then add enough water to cover. Dissolve the bouillon in a little water and add to the saucepan with the cocoa mustard. Season to taste with salt and pepper and cook for 45 minutes.

In a separate saucepan, sauté the peppers in the melted butter with the sugar, then add to the cooked rabbit. Adjust the seasoning if desired. Serve hot.

Indian-style kid masala

Serves 8
Marinate: 2 to 3 hours
Prep: 10 minutes
Cook: 1 hour 10 minutes

1 quantity Meat and Poultry
Marinade (page 242)

4½ lb (2 kg) kid
(goat meat)
----
1 small jar (50g/2 oz)
masala paste
----
1 sprig thyme
----
1 sprig flat-leaf parsley
----
1 bay leaf
----
2 scallions (spring
onions), coarsely chopped
----
1 tablespoon anise seed
----
2 white onions, coarsely
chopped
----
2 cloves garlic, coarsely
chopped
----
2 tablespoons sunflower oil
----
salt and black pepper
----
1 whole chile (chilli)
----
juice of 3 limes

Cut the meat into pieces, brush with the masala paste, then immerse in the marinade. Refrigerate for 2 to 3 hours.

In a blender or food processor, chop the thyme, parsley, bay leaf, scallions, anise, onions and garlic. Heat the oil in a heavy-based saucepan and add the blended herb mixture. Season to taste with salt and pepper. Mix well and gently fry for 5 minutes, adding a little water. Add the drained meat and cover completely with water and the lime juice. Add the whole chile, taking care that it does not burst. Cook over medium heat for an hour.

Serve with lentils and Creole Rice (page 226).

Kid is the most tender and delicate of all goat meat.

Venison stew with guava jelly

Serves 4
Marinate: 2 to 3 hours
Prep: 20 minutes
Cook: 45 minutes

1 quantity Meat and Poultry
Marinade (page 242)

1¾ lb (800 g) venison
fillet, cut into small
pieces
----
2 tablespoons sunflower oil

½ lb (200 g) lardons
----
2 sprigs flat-leaf
parsley, chopped
----
1 onion, chopped
----
3 cloves garlic, chopped
----
1 bay leaf
----
1 rib (stick) celery
----
2 shallots, chopped
----
salt and black pepper
----
1 cup (250 ml/8 fl oz)
red wine
----
2 tablespoons white-wine
vinegar
----
1 carrot, finely sliced
----
4 tablespoons Guava Jelly
(page 314)

Cut the meat into small pieces and marinate in the
refrigerator for 2 to 3 hours.

Heat the oil in a heavy-based saucepan over high
heat and gently fry the drained venison pieces
for 10 minutes. Add the bacon and simmer, stirring
constantly and without adding any water. Add the
parsley, onion, garlic, bay leaf, celery and
shallots. Season to taste with salt and pepper.
Pour in the wine, vinegar and enough water to
cover the meat, then cook over medium heat for 20
minutes more.

Remove the meat from the sauce, strain the sauce,
then return the meat pieces to the sauce and the
heat. Add the carrot and simmer for 15 minutes
more. The sauce should be creamy. Adjust the
seasoning if desired. Serve with the Guava Jelly.

Roast duckling fillets with a Julie mango marmalade

Serves 4
Marinate: 2 to 3 hours
Prep: 10 minutes
Cook: 5 minutes
Roast 15 minutes

1 quantity Meat and Poultry
Marinade (page 242)

----

4 duckling breast fillets,
skins on

----

3 teaspoons sunflower oil

----

salt and black pepper

----

3 Julie mangoes* (if
unavailable, substitute
very ripe mangoes)

----

pinch ground cinnamon

----

pinch cayenne pepper

----

pinch ground cardamom

----

1 tablespoon honey

----

1 tablespoon ground
caraway seeds

----

1 teaspoon ground allspice

----

2 sprigs chervil

Marinate the duck fillets in the refrigerator for
2 to 3 hours.

In a large bowl, combine the oil, salt and pepper.
Add the drained duck fillets and mix well to coat.

Preheat oven to 350°F (180°C/gas 4). Place the
fillets in a roasting pan and roast for 15 minutes.

Peel the mangoes, remove the flesh from the seed
(stone) and purée in a blender or food processor.
Mix the cinnamon, cayenne pepper, cardamom, honey,
caraway and allspice into the purée. Pour into
a saucepan and cook over low heat for 5 minutes.

Serve the duck fillets on the mango marmalade and
garnish the plate with the chopped chervil.

West Indian-style tripe

Serves 6
Prep: 10 minutes
Cook: 10 minutes

3 tablespoons sunflower oil
----
1 sprig flat-leaf parsley
----
scant 1 cup (200 g/7 oz)
chopped very ripe tomatoes

3¼ lb (1.5 kg) precooked
tripe*, finely sliced
----
2 large carrots, sliced
----
11 oz (300 g) smoked
(streaky) bacon, finely
diced
----
2 bay leaves
----
3 cloves garlic, crushed
----
1 sprig thyme, leaves
removed and chopped
----
1 Scotch bonnet chile*
(chilli)

1¾ lb (800 g) ti'figues*,
peeled and sliced
----
salt and black pepper
----
juice of 2 limes
----
2 scallions (spring onions)

Heat the oil in a heavy-based saucepan over low
heat and gently fry the parsley. Add the tomatoes.
Stir well and fry for 5 minutes more. Add the
tripe, carrots, and bacon. Add the bay leaves,
garlic, thyme and whole chile then enough water
to cover. Continue cooking for 10 minutes more.
Set aside.

Stir the ti'figue slices into the tripe mixture.
Mix well. Season to taste with salt and pepper.
Return to the stove and simmer over high heat for
15 minutes. Before serving, add the lime juice and,
if desired, garnish with scallions.

RESTAURAN

MENU LANGOUSTE

- Crudité , accras de morue
Langouste grillée.(riz ou légumes)
- dessert du jour

routard 2004

MENU LANGOUSTE

- Crudité , accras de morue
- Langouste grillée.(riz ou légumes)
dessert du jour

MENU OUASSOUS

- Crudités , accras de morue
- Brochette de ouassous.(riz ou légumes)
- Dessert du jour

20€s

MENU COTE D'AGNEAUX

- Crudités , accras de morue
- Côte d'agneau grillée.(riz ou légumes)
- Dessert du jour

13€

MENU REQUIN

- Crudités   accras de morue
- Brochette de requin.(riz ou
- Dessert du jour

MENU POULET

- Crudités , accras de moru
- Cuisse de poulet.(riz ou l
- Dessert du jour

Excursion dans le lagon

Coco

BOUCHERIE
LA BAVETTE
97.72.08
FRUITS & LÉGUMES
CHARCUTERIE

BOISSONS
GLACES
PLAT DU JOURS

l'Eau à la Bouche

Vegetables . . . or fruit?

Vegetables of the West Indies

1   ti'figue*
2   water lemon
3   banana
4   giraumon*
5   custard apple
6   ambarella*
7   guava
8   star fruit
9   mamoncillo
10 mammee
11 passionfruit
12 plantain*
13 papaya
14 banana flower
15 apple banana
16 plantain*
17 West Indian orange
18 bottle pineapple
19 mango
20 sweet potato
21 coconut
22 wax apple
23 mirliton* (chayote)
24 Guiana chestnut
25 barbadine*
(giant granadilla)
26 achiote
27 madère leaf
28 amaranth (callaloo)
29 pigeon peas*

25

26

27

28

29

Green mango souskai

Serves 4
Prep: 10 minutes
Chill: 3 hours

1 tablespoon sunflower oil
----
1 tablespoon lemon vinegar
(page 156)
----
1 clove garlic, finely
chopped
----
1 sprig cilantro
(coriander), chopped

¼ Scotch bonnet chile*
(chilli), chopped
----
salt and black pepper
----
3 green mangoes, diced
----
pinch superfine (caster)
sugar

Place the oil, vinegar, garlic, cilantro and chile
in a large bowl and mix well. Add the diced mango
and the sugar. Mix well and season to taste with
salt and pepper, if desired. Chill for 3 hours
before serving the souskai*.

Callaloo

Serves 4
Prep: 10 minutes
Cook: 20 minutes

6¾ lb (3 kg) madère
leaves* or spinach, washed
and coarsely chopped

----

4 tablespoons sunflower oil

----

2 cloves garlic, chopped

----

2 onions, chopped

----

2 sprigs flat-leaf
parsley, finely chopped

----

11 oz (300 g) lardons*,

----

salt and black pepper

Bring 1 cup (250 ml/8 fl oz) lightly salted water
to a boil in a Dutch oven or flameproof casserole.
Immerse the madère leaves and cook for 10 minutes.
Drain the leaves, retaining the cooking water, and
immediately plunge the cooked leaves into ice
water so they remain green. Drain, then purée in
a blender or food processor.

Heat the oil in a heavy-based saucepan then gently
fry the garlic, onion and parsley without browning.
Add the lardons and simmer for 2 minutes, stirring
from time to time. Add the leaf purée and half the
cooking water. Season to taste with salt and
pepper. Cook over low heat for 5 minutes more.
Serve hot.

The recipe for this tasty soup comes from Saint Lucia.

Curried cream of yam soup

Serves 4
Prep: 15 minutes
Cook: 25 minutes

1 lb 2 oz (500 g) yams,
peeled and diced

----

juice of 2 limes

----

2 tablespoons olive oil

----

1 onion, chopped

----

2 cloves garlic, chopped

----

1 sprig thyme

----

1 cup (250 ml/8 fl oz)
whole (full-cream) milk

----

2 tablespoons (30 g)
curry powder

----

salt and black pepper

Place the yams in a bowl of water with the lime juice (the lime juice will stop the yams from turning black). Wash the diced yams well in this water, then drain and set aside.

Heat the oil over high heat in a heavy-based saucepan. Fry the onion, garlic and thyme without browning. Add the yam pieces and continue cooking, stirring constantly. Add 4 cups (1 litre/1¾ pints) of water and cook for 20 minutes more.

Purée the mixture in a blender or food processor then return to the saucepan over low heat. Pour in the milk and add the curry powder. Mix well. Season to taste with salt and pepper. Simmer for 2 to 3 minutes. Serve very hot.

Malanga and giraumon acras

Serves 6
Prep: 15 minutes
Chill: 30 minutes
Cook: 3 minutes

1⅓ cups (300 g/11 oz)
peeled and grated malanga*
(if unavailable,
substitute sweet potatoes)
----
scant 1 cup (200 g/7 oz)
peeled and grated
giraumon*
----
1 onion, finely chopped
----
1 clove garlic, finely
chopped
----
2 scallions (spring
onions), chopped
----
1 sprig flat-leaf parsley,
chopped
----
2 eggs

¼ Scotch bonnet chile*
(chilli), finely chopped
----
salt and black pepper

1½ teaspoons baking powder
----
4 cups (1 litre/1¾ pints)
sunflower oil, for
deep-frying

In a large bowl, mix the grated malanga and
giraumon with the onion, garlic, scallions,
parsley, eggs and chile. Season to taste with
salt and pepper. Mix well then refrigerate for
30 minutes. Just before making the acras, add
the baking powder and stir vigorously.

Heat the oil in a deep-fryer or large saucepan.
When very hot, drop in teaspoonfuls of the mixture
and fry until golden. The acras will take shape
and rise to the surface of the oil. Remove from
oil, drain on paper towels and serve hot.

Féroce

This style of avocado purée is popular on the island of Martinique.

Serves 4
Soak: 24 hours
Prep: 10 minutes

7 oz (200 g) salt cod
----
1 clove garlic
----
1 sprig flat-leaf parsley
----
2 shallots
----
2 scallions (spring onions)
----
pinch chili powder
----
2 avocados
----
2 oz (50 g) cassava* (tapioca) flour
----
1 lime
----
3 tablespoons sunflower oil
----
salt and black pepper

Place the salt cod in a large bowl of cool water to soak overnight. The next day, place the cod in a saucepan of water and boil vigorously over high heat. Drain the water and repeat several times. When the fish is completely rehydrated, drain and break it into pieces. Coarsely chop the fish pieces in a blender or food processor then transfer to a large bowl and set aside.

In the blender or food processor, chop the garlic, parsley, shallots, scallions and chili powder, then add to the large bowl.

Cut the avocados in half lengthwise and remove the flesh, retaining the skins. Purée the flesh in the blender or food processor until very smooth, then add to the large bowl.

Using a wooden spoon, mix the avocado purée, cod and chopped herb mixture. Add the lime juice and oil. Season to taste with salt and pepper and mix well. Add the cassava flour and stir until the mixture is very smooth.

Fill the retained avocado skins with the mixture and, if desired, serve on a bed of sliced cucumbers dressed with lime juice.

Yam croquettes

Serves 4
Prep: 15 minutes
Cook: 5 minutes

1 onion
----
1 sprig flat-leaf parsley

2¼ lb (1 kg) white yams*,
peeled and grated
----
2 egg yolks
----
salt and black pepper
----
4 cups (1 litre/1¾ pints)
sunflower oil, for deep-
frying

In a blender or food processor, finely chop the
onion and the parsley and place in a bowl. Add the
grated yam and the egg yolks, and season to taste
with salt and pepper. Mix vigorously.

Heat the oil in a large saucepan until very hot.
Drop table-spoonfuls of the yam purée into the oil
and cook until golden on all sides. Drain on paper
towels before serving.

Yam fries

Serves 4
Prep: 10 minutes
Cook: 5 minutes

9 oz (250 g) white yams*

----

white-wine vinegar

----

4 cups (1 litre/1¾ pints)
sunflower oil, for
deep-frying

----

salt and black pepper

Peel the yams and cut lengthwise into ⅜-in
(8 mm)-wide strips. Soak in water with a little
vinegar until the moment you fry them. Drain then
pat dry using a clean cloth.

Heat the oil until very hot. Immerse the yams and
fry until golden. Drain. Season to taste with salt,
pepper and, if desired, vinegar.

Grandmother's giraumon

Serves 4
Prep: 10 minutes
Cook: 15 to 20 minutes

2 scallions (spring onions)
----
1 sprig flat-leaf parsley
----
1 sprig thyme
----
2 white onions
----
3 cloves garlic

¼ cup (50 ml) sunflower oil

2¼ lb (1 kg) giraumon*,
peeled and chopped
----
a grating fresh ginger
----
salt and black pepper

In a blender or food processor, chop the scallions, parsley, thyme, onions and garlic. Set aside.

Heat the oil in a heavy-based saucepan then gently fry the giraumon pieces. Add the chopped herb mixture and the ginger. Mix well and cook over high heat for 5 minutes. Season to taste with salt and pepper.

Lower the heat and continue cooking, stirring constantly, for 10 minutes more, until the giraumon becomes a purée. Serve hot.

Yellow banana bake

Serves 4
Prep: 10 minutes
Cook: 5 minutes
Bake: 20 to 25 minutes

2¼ lb (1 kg) very ripe
plantains*
----
4 teaspoons (20 g/¾ oz)
butter
----
2 to 3 tablespoons all-
purpose (plain) flour
----
2 cups (500 ml/18 fl oz)
whole (full-cream) milk
----
pinch ground cinnamon
----
salt and black pepper
----
3 tablespoons grated
cheese (such as gruyère)

Cut the plantains in half. Peel them then cut
each half lengthwise into fine slices. Set aside.

Preheat oven to 350°F (180°C/gas 4). Melt the
butter in a saucepan. Add the flour and mix well.
Slowly pour in the milk, stirring constantly. Add
the cinnamon. Season to taste with salt and pepper.
The béchamel is ready.

Grease and flour a baking dish. Arrange the
plantain slices in the dish in layers. Top with
the béchamel, taking care that it penetrates all
the layers of plantain. Sprinkle with the cheese
and bake for 20 to 25 minutes.

Kidney-bean Creole consommé

Serves 4
Soak: 12 to 24 hours
Prep: 5 minutes
Cook: 3 hours 30 minutes

1 lb 2 oz (500 g) dried
kidney beans
----
3 bay leaves
----
2 sprigs thyme
----
3 scallions (spring
onions), chopped
----
1 red onion, chopped
----
2 cloves garlic, chopped
----
3 whole cloves
----
3 tablespoons sunflower oil
----
salt and black pepper
----
1 quantity Creole Rice
(page 226)

The day before serving, soak the kidney beans in
3 quarts (3 litres/5 pints) water in a Dutch oven
or stock pot. The next day, cook the beans over
high heat for 2 hours 30 minutes. Add the bay
leaves, thyme and scallions. Stir in the onion,
garlic, cloves and oil. Season to taste with salt
and pepper.

Reduce the heat to low and continue cooking until
the beans become creamy. If their consistency is
still not good, take a ladleful of the beans,
purée them in a blender or food processor, then
return them to the pan. Stir well and serve with
Creole Rice.

Pigeon-pea Creole consommé

Serves 4
Prep: 5 minutes
Cook: 40 minutes

2 tablespoons sunflower oil

----

1 lb 2 oz (500 g) shelled
pigeon peas*, rinsed

----

7 oz (200 g) lardons*

----

2 sprigs thyme, finely
chopped

----

3 sprigs flat-leaf
parsley, finely chopped

----

2 white onions, finely
chopped

----

3 scallions (spring
onions), finely chopped

----

1 bay leaf

----

salt and black pepper

Heat the oil in a heavy-based saucepan and add the peas. Mix well, then add the lardons and fry for 10 minutes, stirring constantly. Add 6 cups (1.5 litres/2½ pints) water. Add the thyme, parsley, onions, scallions and bay leaf. Season to taste with salt and pepper. Cover and cook over high heat for 30 minutes. At the end of the cooking time, the mixture should be creamy, with very little liquid.Serve hot.

Yam purée with saffron threads

Serves 4
Prep: 10 minutes
Cook: 20 minutes

2¼ lb (1 kg) white yams*,
peeled and chopped

----

2 oz (50 g) butter

----

salt and black pepper

----

1 tablespoon olive oil

½ teaspoon saffron threads

----

1 cup (250 ml/8 fl oz)
whole (full-cream) milk

Bring 4 cups (1 litre/1¾ pints) salted water to a
boil; cook yams for 15 minutes. Drain.

In a blender or food processor, purée the yams
then transfer to a saucepan over low heat. Add the
butter and milk and mix well. Season to taste with
salt and pepper. Add the olive oil and saffron.
Mix well then serve hot.

Creole rice

Serves 4
Prep: 2 minutes
Cook: 12 minutes

scant 1 cup (200 g/7 oz)
long-grain rice or jasmine
rice, rinsed
----
pinch salt
----
1 tablespoon sunflower oil

Put the rice a saucepan and add enough water to come ¼ in (5 mm) above the rice. Add the salt, mix well, bring to a boil, then cook, covered, over medium heat for 12 minutes. The rice should absorb all the water. At the end of cooking, add in the oil and mix well.

Lentils mixed with rice

Serves 4
Prep: 10 minutes
Cook: 60 minutes

scant 1 cup (200 g/7 oz)
green lentils
----
1 sprig thyme
----
1 sprig flat-leaf parsley,
chopped
----
1 onion, chopped
----
7 oz (200 g) lardons*
----
2 whole cloves
----
3 bay leaves

1⅓ cups (300 g/11 oz)
long-grain rice, rinsed
----
salt and black pepper
----
3 tablespoons sunflower oil

Place the lentils in a Dutch oven or stock pot containing 2 quarts (2 litres/3½ pints) of water, bring to a boil and cook, covered, over high heat for 30 minutes.

Add the thyme, parsley, onion, lardons, cloves and bay leaves. Cook for 10 minutes more, then add the rice. Season to taste with salt and pepper. Add water if necessary to just cover the rice; if there is too much water, remove the surplus. Cook over medium heat for 20 minutes more, then add the oil and stir well. Serve hot.

Rice mixed with kidney beans

Serves 4
Soak: 12 to 24 hours
Prep: 15 minutes
Cook: 2 hours 45 minutes

scant 1 cup (200 g/7 oz)
dried kidney beans

----

1 bay leaf

----

3 whole cloves

----

1 sprig flat-leaf parsley,
chopped

----

1 sprig thyme

----

7 oz (200 g) lardons*

----

1 onion, chopped

----

2 cloves garlic

1⅓ cups (300 g/11 oz)
jasmine rice, rinsed

----

salt and black pepper

----

3 tablespoons sunflower oil

The day before serving, soak the kidney beans in
a Dutch oven or stock pot containing a gallon
(4 litres/7 pints) of water.

The next day, place the Dutch oven directly on the
stove, add the bay leaf, cloves, parsley and thyme,
then cover and cook over high heat for 2 hours.
Add the lardons and the onion and garlic. Cook for
30 minutes more.

When the beans are soft, add the rice to the pan.
Add enough water to come 1 in (2.5 cm) above the
level of the rice. Mix well using a wooden spoon.
Add salt if desired and season to taste with
pepper, then simmer over low heat for 15 minutes,
stirring occasionally so that the rice doesn't
stick to the pan. Remove from heat and add the oil.
Serve hot.

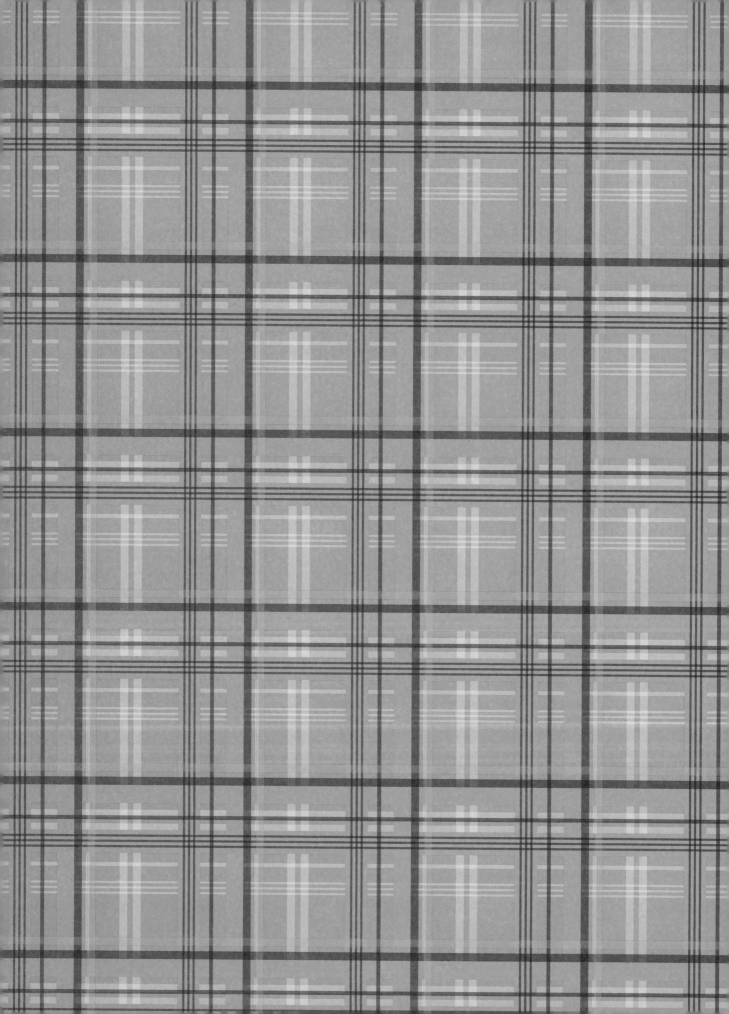

Sauces

Saffron seafood 'cream'

Serves 4
Prep: 10 minutes
Cook: 20 minutes

3½ oz (100 g) cockles*
(if unavailable, substitute
hard-shell clams)

3½ oz (100 g)
Dublin Bay prawns
(if unavailable,
substitute jumbo shrimp)
----
1 tablespoon olive oil
----
1 shallot, finely chopped
----
1 clove garlic, finely
chopped
----
2 oz (50 g) crabmeat
----
1 cup (250 ml/8 fl oz)
dry white wine
----
juice of 1 lime
----
1 bird's-eye chile*
(chilli), finely chopped
(if unavailable, substitute
piquin or serrano chile)
----
salt and black pepper
----
pinch ground turmeric

½ teaspoon saffron threads
----
2 tablespoons sunflower oil

Cook then shell the cockles. (The shells can
be prised open, using a blunt knife or similar
instrument, on the sharp side of the shell and by
levering the two halves apart.) Shell and devein
the prawns, removing the heads.

Heat the 2 tablespoons of sunflower oil in a heavy-
based saucepan then gently fry the shallots and
garlic. Add the cockles, prawns and crabmeat, then
simmer for 2 to 3 minutes. Pour in the white wine
and the lime juice. Add the chile. Mix well then
cook for 3 minutes more.

Purée the cooked mixture in a blender or food
pro-cessor for 1 to 2 minutes then pass through
a strainer. Return the purée to the saucepan over
high heat. Season to taste with salt and pepper.
Add the turmeric, saffron and olive oil. Cook for
2 minutes more. Serve hot.

Spicy onion sauce

Serves 4
Prep: 10 minutes
Cook: 30 minutes

3 tablespoons olive oil

1¾ lb (800 g) red onions,
finely sliced

----

salt and black pepper

----

pinch ground cumin

----

pinch quatre épices*

¼ cup (50 ml/2 fl oz) honey

----

3 tablespoons sherry
vinegar

----

1 chile (chilli), chopped

Heat the oil in a heavy-based saucepan, then add
the onions. Season to taste with salt and pepper.
Mix well. Add the cumin and quatre épices then
cook, covered, for 30 minutes over low heat.
Stir from time to time.

Remove from heat and add the honey, sherry vinegar,
chile and 2 tablespoons water. Mix well then purée
in a blender or food processor.

Spicy Sweet and Sour sauce

Serves 4
Prep: 10 minutes
Chill: 2 hours

2 sprigs cilantro
(coriander), finely chopped
----
2 sprigs flat-leaf parsley,
finely chopped
----
1 clove garlic, peeled,
finely chopped
----
1 shallot, finely chopped
----
pinch chili powder
----
2 tablespoons sunflower oil
----
juice of 3 oranges
----
juice of 2 limes
----
salt and black pepper

Mix the cilantro, parsley, garlic, shallot and chili powder in a large bowl with the oil and the citrus juices. Season to taste with salt and pepper. Stir well and let stand in the refrigerator for 2 hours before serving. This sauce is served cold and is the ideal accompaniment for grilled meats.

Babette's fiery sauce

Serves 4
Prep: 10 minutes

1 very ripe tomato,
coarsely chopped

----

1 clove garlic, coarsely
chopped

----

2 sprigs flat-leaf
parsley, coarsely chopped

----

1 Scotch bonnet chile*
(chilli)

----

5 tablespoons sunflower oil

----

juice of 3 limes

----

salt and black pepper

Purée the tomato, garlic, parsley, chile, oil and 3 tablespoons water in a blender or food processor. Pour the mixture into a bowl, add the lime juice and season to taste with salt and pepper. Serve this sauce with meat, poultry and fish.

West Indian tomato sauce with ginger

Serves 4
Prep: 10 minutes

4 very ripe tomatoes

----

3 tablespoons sunflower oil

----

pinch chili powder

----

2 teaspoons chopped fresh
ginger

----

salt and black pepper

Bring a saucepan of water to a boil then immerse the tomatoes for 1 minute. Drain, peel and deseed. Purée the tomato flesh in a blender or food processor with the oil, chili powder and ginger. Season to taste with salt and pepper. Mix well. Keep the sauce in an airtight jar in the refrigerator.

Traditional 'Sauce chien'

Serves 6
Prep: 10 minutes

juice of 4 limes
----
2 tablespoons sunflower oil
----
3 sprigs flat-leaf
parsley, chopped
----
4 cloves garlic, chopped

½ Scotch bonnet chile*
(chilli), chopped
----
6 scallions (spring
onions), chopped

In a large bowl, combine the lime juice, oil,
parsley, scallions, garlic and chile. Mix well.

Pour ⅔ cup (150 ml/¼ pint) boiling water over the
lime juice mixture. Cover the bowl with a clean
cloth and let stand to infuse until completely
cooled. Serve cold with meat and grilled fish.

This sauce got its name from the West Indian phrase 'c'est chien', used to describe something that tastes delicious.

Creole mayonnaise

Serves 4
Prep: 10 minutes

1 egg yolk
----
1 tablespoon strong
mustard
----
1 cup (250 ml/8 fl oz)
garlic-infused olive oil
----
salt and black pepper
----
1 sprig cilantro
(coriander)
----
pinch chili powder
----
juice of 1 lime
----
juice of ½ orange

Place the egg yolk and the mustard in a bowl.
Pour in the oil a little at a time, whisking gently
to form a mayonnaise. Once all the oil is added,
season to taste with salt and pepper. In a blender
or food processor, chop the cilantro with the chili
powder; stir into the mayonnaise, along with the
citrus juices. Mix well.

Fish marinade

For 2¼ lb (1 kg) fish
Prep: 10 minutes

salt and black pepper
----
1 Scotch bonnet chile*
(chilli), chopped
----
3 cloves garlic, coarsely
chopped
----
1 onion, coarsely chopped
----
2 tablespoons white-wine
vinegar
----
4 limes

Place the fish to be marinated in a large bowl
and cover with water. Season with salt and pepper.
Add the chile, garlic, onion and vinegar. Chop the
limes into pieces, squeeze them into the bowl then
add the pieces to the bowl. Cover and chill for 8
hours to marinate. The marinade will permeate the
flesh of the fish and, after cooking, it will have
a unique and excellent taste.

Meat and poultry marinade

For 2¼ lb (1 kg) meat
or poultry
Prep: 10 minutes

1 onion, chopped
----
2 cloves garlic, chopped
----
pinch ground cumin
----
salt and black pepper
----
2 tablespoons sunflower oil
----
2 tablespoons white-wine
vinegar

Chop the meat or poultry into pieces then place in
a deep container. Add the onion and garlic, then
the cumin. Season with salt and pepper. Pour in the
oil and vinegar. Mix well, cover and chill for 2 to
3 hours before cooking.

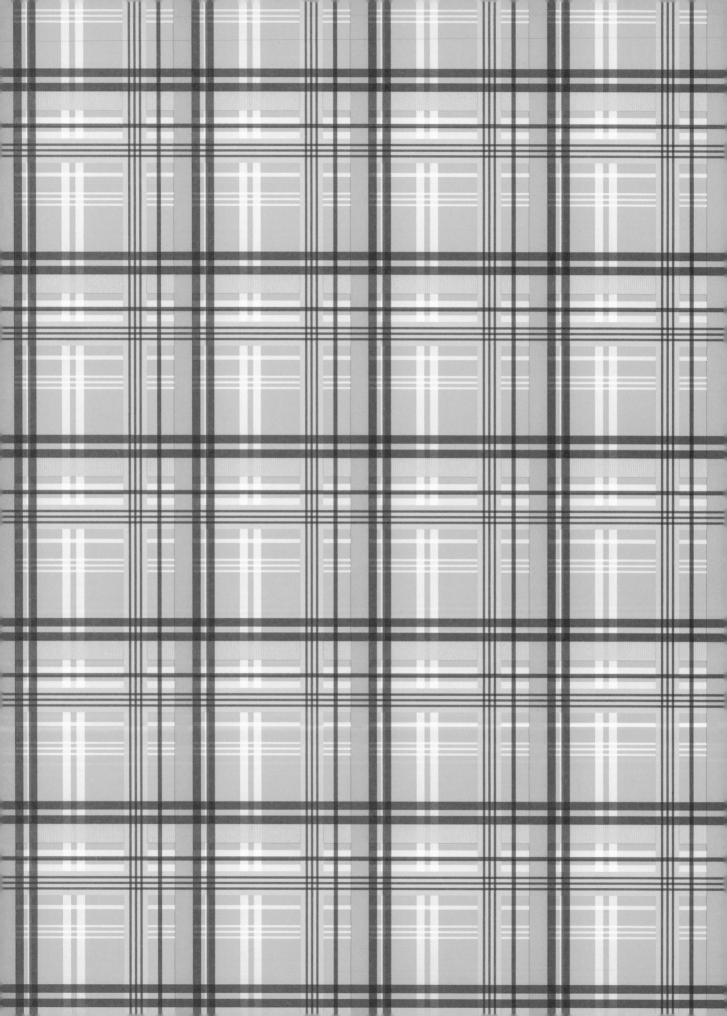

Desserts
and sweets

Flambé of roasted bananas with lime zest

Serves 4
Prep: 10 minutes
Cook: 8 minutes

4 tablespoons superfine (caster) sugar

----

4 very ripe, black-spotted bananas, peeled

----

juice of 2 oranges

----

juice of 1 lime plus several large strips of zest

----

1 cinnamon stick

¼ cup (50 ml/2 fl oz) aged rum (rhum vieux)

Put the sugar in a saucepan over high heat. When it caramelizes, add the bananas and the citrus juices. Add the reserved lime zest and the cinnamon stick. Reduce the heat and allow to cook gently for 3 to 4 minutes, turning the bananas so that they become golden all over. Pour in the rum; set aflame before serving, gently shaking the pan.

Mardi Gras beignets with vanilla

Serves 6
Prep: 10 minutes
Cook: 3 minutes

9 oz (250 g) all-purpose (plain) flour, sifted

---

2 eggs, separated

---

5 oz (150 g) superfine (caster) sugar

---

grated zest of 1 lime

---

1 tablespoon ground vanilla (if unavailable, substitute 2 tablespoons pure vanilla extract)

½ tablespoon ground cinnamon

---

pinch nutmeg

---

2 tablespoons (25 g/1 oz) butter, melted

---

scant ⅓ cup (60 ml/3 fl oz) aged rum (rhum vieux)

---

pinch salt

---

4 cups (1 litre/1¾ pints) sunflower oil, for deep-frying

---

scant ½ cup (100 g) powdered (icing) sugar, for dusting

Place the flour, egg yolks, sugar and a scant ½ cup (100 ml/3½ fl oz) water in a large bowl. Mix gently. Add the lime zest, vanilla, cinnamon, nutmeg, melted butter and rum. Mix well and set aside.

Beat the egg whites with pinch of salt until stiff peaks form. Fold into the rum mixture to form a smooth paste without any lumps.

Heat the oil in a large saucepan. Drop in teaspoonfuls of the mixture. Once the fritters are golden, drain and place on paper towels. Serve hot, sprinkled with powdered sugar.

During carnival time, Mardi Gras is a day of general jubilation for West Indians. Traditionally, merchants sell beignets in all the streets.

Mango and pineapple bisque flavored with rum

Serves 6
Stand: 8 to 24 hours
Prep: 10 minutes
Cook: 10 minutes
Chill: 12 to 24 hours

1 4-to-4½-lb (2 kg) pineapple, diced

----

3 Julie mangoes*, peeled and chopped

⅓ cup (80 g/3 oz) cane sugar or white sugar

----

pinch ground cinnamon

----

3 tablespoons aged rum (rhum vieux)

----

4 cups (1 litre/1¾ pints) whole (full-cream) milk

¼ cup (50 ml/2 fl oz) crème fraîche (see page 62)

----

a few fresh mint leaves

Two days before serving, make the crème fraîche. Partially cover and let stand 8 to 24 hours or until very thick. (The crème fraîche will keep, covered, in the refrigerator for up to 10 days.)

The next day, purée the pineapple and mango in a blender or food processor. Put the sugar and cinnamon in a saucepan and cook over high heat until the mixture is caramelized. Stir in the rum and the milk, then the puréed pineapple and mango. Bring to a simmer then cook over low heat for 5 minutes. Pass the soup through a strainer. Add the crème fraîche and mix well.

Set aside to cool, then chill overnight. Serve with a garnish of mint leaves.

Coconut blancmange

Serves 4
Stand: 8 to 24 hours
Prep: 20 minutes
Cook: 5 minutes
Chill: 12 to 24 hours

8 gelatin leaves
(if unavailable,
substitute ½ oz/15 g
granulated gelatin)
----
1 cup (250 ml/8 fl oz)
whole (full-cream) milk
----
14 fl oz (400 ml)
coconut milk
----
1 ½ cups (350 ml/12 fl oz)
crème fraîche (see page 62)
----
scant 1 cup (200 g/7 oz)
superfine (caster) sugar

Two days before serving, make the crème fraîche.
Partially cover and let stand 8 to 24 hours or
until very thick. (The crème fraîche will keep,
covered, in the refrigerator for up to 10 days.)

The next day, soak the gelatin leaves in a little
water to soften.

Bring the milk to a boil in a saucepan over medium
heat. Add the softened and drained gelatin leaves
and stir to combine. Pour in the coconut milk. Cook
for 3 minutes, stirring occasionally. Remove from
heat and set aside to cool completely.

Place the crème fraîche and sugar in a large bowl.
Using an electric mixer, whip the cream until soft
peaks begin to form. Slowly beat in the cooled milk
mixture. Pour into 1 dish or 4 individual ramekins
and refrigerate overnight before serving.

Four-spice and ginger cake

Serves 6
Prep: 10 minutes
Bake: 45 minutes

8 eggs

---

scant 1 cup (200 g/7 oz)
sugar

---

pinch salt

---

9 oz (250 g) butter,
softened

---

1 teaspoon ground vanilla
(if unavailable,
substitute 2 teaspoons
pure vanilla extract)

---

9 oz (250 g) all-purpose
(plain) flour

---

4 teaspoons baking powder

---

2 teaspoons ground
cinnamon

---

scant 1 cup (200 g/7 oz)
candied (crystallised)
ginger

---

5 oz (150 g) currants

---

3 tablespoons quatre
épices*

---

2 ground cloves

Preheat oven to 350°F (180°C/gas 4).

Break the eggs into the bowl of an electric mixer.
Add the sugar and the salt. Mix at low speed until
the mixture is light and fluffy. Add the butter,
then the vanilla. Mix in the flour, baking powder,
cinnamon, ginger, currants, quatre épices and
ground cloves. Mix well.

Pour the mixture into a buttered cake pan. Bake for
45 minutes.

Crème brulée with sirop de batterie

Serves 4
Stand: 8 to 24 hours
Prep: 15 minutes
Bake: 45 minutes
Broil: 3 minutes

1 vanilla bean (pod)

----

3 egg yolks

⅓ cup (80 ml/3 fl oz)
sirop de batterie*

1¼ cups (300 ml/½ pint)
thick crème fraîche
(see page 62)

----

2 cups (500 ml/18 fl oz)
whole (full-cream) milk

----

3 tablespoons brown sugar

The day before serving, make the crème fraîche.
Partially cover and let stand 8 to 24 hours or
until very thick. (The crème fraîche will keep,
covered, in the refrigerator for up to 10 days.)

The next day, split the vanilla bean lengthwise
with a knife then scrape the insides with the knife
tip to remove the small black seeds. Place the egg
yolks, sirop de batterie, crème fraîche and vanilla
seeds in a bowl. Beat well. Mix in the milk then
set aside for 15 minutes.

Preheat oven to 350°F (180°C/gas 4). Pour the
mixture into 4 individual ramekins. Bake in a bain
marie* (water bath) for about 45 minutes. Allow to
cool, then sprinkle with brown sugar.

Place the ramekins under a preheated broiler
(grill) for 3 minutes. When the sugar is well
caramelized, chill for at least an hour before
serving.

Coconut flans in caramel sauce

Serves 4
Stand: 8 to 24 hours
Prep: 15 minutes
Bake: 1 hour
Chill: 12 to 24 hours

2 eggs

¼ cup (50 ml/2 fl oz)
thick crème fraîche
(see page 62)

----

scant ½ cup (100 ml/
3½ fl oz) coconut milk

----

scant ½ cup (100 ml/
3½ fl oz) sweetened
condensed milk

----

2 tablespoons desiccated
coconut

----

1 tablespoon (15 g/½ oz)
butter

Caramel

1 vanilla bean (pod)

----

2 tablespoons cane sugar
or white (caster) sugar

----

juice of 1 lime

¼ cup (50 ml/2 fl oz) aged
rum (rhum vieux)

----

juice of 2 oranges

Two days before serving, make the crème fraîche.
Partially cover and let stand 8 to 24 hours or
until very thick. (The crème fraîche will keep,
covered, in the refrigerator for up to 10 days.)

The next day, prepare the caramel: split the
vanilla bean lengthwise with a knife then scrape
the insides with the knife tip to remove the small
black seeds. Place the sugar, the lime juice and
the vanilla seeds in a saucepan. Let the mixture
caramelize, then slowly add the rum. Add the orange
juice and allow to thicken.

Preheat oven to 350°F (180°C/gas 4). Beat the eggs
then, still beating, add the crème fraîche,
coconut milk and condensed milk. Add 1 teaspoon
of the desiccated coconut. Butter 4 ramekins and
pour a little of the caramel sauce into each,
retaining the remaining sauce, then fill with the
coconut mixture.

Bake in a bain marie* (water bath) for 1 hour. When
the desserts are cooked, remove from oven and allow
to cool before turning out. Refrigerate overnight.

Serve the flans topped with the rest of the caramel
and, if desired, sprinkled with the remaining
desiccated coconut.

Mango fricassee parcels

Serves 4
Prep: 10 minutes
Cook: 15 minutes
Bake: 5 minutes

2 tablespoons (25 g/1 oz)
unsalted butter

---

scant ½ cup (100 g/3½ oz)
cane sugar or white
(caster) sugar

---

juice of 4 oranges, plus
strips of zest for garnish

---

juice of 2 limes, plus
strips of zest for garnish

---

2 strips lime zest, finely
sliced

---

5 mangoes, peeled and cut
into large pieces

---

a grating nutmeg

---

2 cinnamon sticks

---

4 tablespoons aged rum
(rhum vieux)

---

4 sheets phyllo dough
(filo pastry), folded into
6-inch squares

---

a few glacé cherries

---

a few mint leaves, chopped

Heat the butter in a skillet or frying pan over
low heat. Add the sugar and cook until caramelized.
Add the orange and lime juices and the lime zest.
Mix well then add the mango pieces, the nutmeg and
cinnamon. Simmer over low heat for 10 minutes to
reduce the sauce.

Preheat oven to 500°F (260°C/gas 10). Add the rum
to the mango mixture and set it aflame, gently
shaking the pan. Remove the mango from the sauce
and set aside. Place 2 mango pieces in the middle
of each phyllo square. Fold up the edges of the
pastry, gather together at the top and hold shut
with a toothpick. Bake for 5 minutes.

Pour a little of the retained sauce into each
serving dish, then place a mango parcel on top.
Garnish with the glacé cherries and the chopped mint
leaves, and with strips of lime and orange zest.

Cocoa

Soft chocolate gateau

Serves 4
Prep: 20 minutes
Cook: 10 minutes
Bake: 45 minutes

5 oz (150 g) semi-sweet
(plain) chocolate, broken
into pieces

1¼ cups (300 ml/½ pint)
whole (full-cream) milk

4¼ oz (125 g/4 oz)
unsalted butter

----

3 eggs, separated

4½ oz (130 g) superfine
(caster) sugar

----

pinch salt

4¼ oz (125 g) all-purpose
(plain) flour, sifted

----

powdered (icing) sugar,
for dusting

Place the chocolate and milk in the top of a double
boiler or in an oven-proof bowl on top of a
saucepan of hot water. Stir until the chocolate
melts. Cut the butter into cubes and melt in another
saucepan, over low heat for 2 to 3 minutes.

Beat the egg yolks in a bowl with the sugar until
the mixture is pale and fluffy. In a separate bowl,
beat the egg whites with the salt until very stiff.
Fold the sifted flour into the whites, then add
the melted chocolate, then the beaten yolks.
Mix carefully.

Preheat oven to 375°F (190°C/gas 5). Pour the mixture into a buttered cake pan and bake for 45
minutes. Let cool completely before turning out and
dusting with powdered sugar. If desired, serve the
gateau topped with vanilla ice cream or custard.

Soft sweet potato cake with a coulis of exotic fruits

Serves 6
Prep: 20 minutes
Cook: 15 minutes
Bake: 15 minutes

4 sweet potatoes
----

juice and grated zest of
2 limes
----

grated zest of 2 oranges
----

1 vanilla bean (pod)
----

3 eggs
----

5 oz (150 g) superfine
(caster) sugar
----

9 oz (250 g) butter
----

pinch ground cinnamon
----

orange flower water
----

2 tablespoons aged rum
(rhum vieux)
----

1 teaspoon vanilla extract
----

flour, for dusting
----

1 mango
----

1 kiwi

½ Victoria pineapple
----

2 passionfruit
----

2 star fruit

½ papaya

Cut off the ends of the sweet potatoes and peel the remainder. Squeeze the juice of 1 limes into cold water and immerse the sweet potatoes for a few seconds so they don't blacken. Cut the sweet potatoes into large, regular pieces and place in a large saucepan with plenty of salted cold water.

Add the orange and lime zest, along with the whole vanilla bean. Bring to a boil, cook for about 15 minutes or until sweet potatoes are cooked through, then drain. Remove the vanilla and purée the sweet potatoes and citrus zest in a blender or food processor. Transfer purée to a large bowl.

One by one, add the eggs, then the sugar, beating well with each addition. Melt the butter and add, stirring well. Add the cinnamon, a few drops of orange flower water, rum and vanilla extract. Finish with the juice of the remaining lime, then beat well until the purée is very smooth.

Preheat oven to 300°F (150°C/gas 2). Grease and flour a cake pan. Pour in the sweet potato mixture and bake for 15 minutes.

Turn out the cake and serve, preferably warm, accompanied by a cold thick purée, or coulis, made by blending exotic fruits such as mango, kiwi, pineapple, passionfruit, starfruit and papaya, in a blender or food processor. Decorate with vanilla beans.

Sweet potato slice

Serves 4
Prep: 15 minutes
Cook: 35 minutes
Bake: 15 minutes

2 rolls puff (flaky) pastry
----
scant 1 cup (200 g/7 oz)
sweet potato, peeled and
diced
----
2 cups (500 ml/18 fl oz)
whole (full-cream) milk
----
11 oz (300 g) superfine
(caster) sugar
----
2 vanilla beans (pods)
zest of 1 lime
----
1 cinnamon stick
----
6 egg yolks
----
scant ½ cup (100 g/3½ oz)
all-purpose (plain) flour
----
2 tablespoons ground
almonds

4½ tablespoons (60 g/2½ oz)
butter
----
2 tablespoons powdered
(icing) sugar, for
sprinkling

Preheat oven to 350°F (180°C/gas 4).

Spread out the pastry on a lightly floured work
surface. Cut into 6 identical rectangles and prick
with a fork. Arrange the rectangles on a baking
sheet, then cover with a baking pan filled with pie
(pastry) weights, to prevent too much swelling.
Bake for 15 minutes.

In a saucepan, cook the sweet potatoes in 1 cup
(250 ml/8 fl oz) of the milk. Add a scant ½ cup
(100 g/3½ oz) of the sugar, 1 of the vanilla beans,
the lime zest and the cinnamon stick, then cook for
15 to 20 minutes. Drain, remove vanilla bean and
cinnamon stick, then mash using a fork.

In another saucepan, bring the remaining milk to
a boil with the remaining vanilla bean. Meanwhile,
mix the egg yolks with the remaining sugar in a
large bowl. Add the mashed sweet potato, the flour
and the ground almonds. Pour in the boiling milk
and beat vigorously. Return the mixture to a
saucepan and cook over low heat for 2 to 3 minutes
more. Remove from heat, add the butter and beat
vigorously until very smooth and creamy. Set aside
to cool.

Begin putting the slices together. Cover a
rectangle of cooked puff pastry with a layer of the
sweet potato cream. Add another rectangle of pastry
and repeat, ending with a rectangle of puff pastry,
then sprinkle with powdered sugar. Serve with a
sweet potato coulis, garnished with a few chopped
mint leaves.

Mango and passionfruit mousse

Serves 6
Prep: 20 minutes
Chill: 12 to 24 hours

2 gelatin leaves
(if unavailable,
substitute ⅛ oz/3 g
granulated gelatin)
----
2 very ripe mangoes
(about 18 oz/500 g flesh)
----
6 passionfruit
----
scant 1 cup (200 g/7 oz)
superfine (caster) sugar
----
grated zest of 1 lime
----
2 tablespoons passionfruit
syrup
----
12 mint leaves
----
1 papaya, peeled and sliced

The day before serving, place the gelatin leaves
in a bowl of cold water to soften. Purée the mango
flesh in a blender or food processor; set aside.
Halve the passionfruit, then empty each half using
a teaspoon. Purée the pulp (including the seeds)
in a blender or food processor with a small glass
of water. Pass through a sieve to remove any trace
of seeds.

Pour the passionfruit purée into a bowl and add
the sugar. Mix well. Add the lime zest, mango purée
and drained gelatin leaves. Stir well until the
gelatin is completely combined. Add the passionfruit syrup, then purée the mixture in the blender
or food processor.

Place a few mint leaves at the bottom of 6 glasses,
then some papaya slices, then the mango mousse.
Refrigerate overnight. Serve cold.

Coconut mini spring rolls with a Victoria Pineapple coulis

Serves 4
Prep: 35 minutes
Cook: 2 minutes

1 coconut

----

2 tablespoons (25 g/1 oz)
butter

----

scant 1 cup (200 g/7 oz)
brown sugar

----

1 vanilla bean (pod),
split lengthwise

----

pinch ground cinnamon

----

pinch freshly ground
nutmeg

----

1 thick strip lime zest

----

10 rice spring-roll
wrappers

----

1 Victoria pineapple,
peeled and cut into thin
strips (if unavailable,
substitute another variety
of pineapple)

----

4 cups (1 litre/1¾ pints)
sunflower oil, for
deep-frying

----

2 tablespoons powdered
(icing) sugar, for
sprinkling

Break open the coconut and grate finely, reserving a little for garnish.

Melt the butter in a saucepan with the brown sugar. Stir and allow to caramelize a little, then add the grated coconut. Cook, stirring constantly, for 2 to 3 minutes, then add 1 cup (250 ml/8 fl oz) water. Add the vanilla bean, the cinnamon, nutmeg and lime zest. Stir, then add another 1 cup (250 ml/8 fl oz) water. Cook over low heat for 15 to 20 minutes more, until the mixture forms a creamy jam. Remove from heat and set aside to cool.

Soften the spring roll wrappers in a clean, damp cloth. When they are very supple, spread them out on the work surface. Place a little of the pineapple on each, then a small heap of the coconut jam. Roll up one by one and let them sit at room temperature for 5 to 8 minutes. Heat the oil in a large saucepan until very hot, then fry the rolls, stirring occasionally so they brown all over. Drain on paper towels.

Arrange on a bed of grated coconut and sprinkle with powdered sugar. If desired, serve with a thick purée, or coulis, made from pineapple, pulped in a blender or food processor. Garnish with mint leaves, if desired.

Papaya salad with strawberries, mint and mandarins

Serves 4
Prep: 10 minutes

2 ripe papayas
----
scant 1 cup (200 g/7 oz)
strawberries, hulled
----
3 tablespoons superfine
(caster) sugar
----
juice of 1 mandarin orange
----
2 tablespoons white rum
----
5 mint leaves, chopped

Peel the papayas and cut in half. Carefully remove and reserve the seeds using a teaspoon, then dice or finely slice the flesh.

Place the strawberries, sugar, mandarin juice, rum and chopped mint in a blender or food processor. Purée well then pour over the papaya. Garnish with papaya seeds and serve cold.

Love's torment

Serves 6
Prep: 1 hour
Cook: 35 minutes
Bake: 20 minutes

This dish comes from Les Saintes Islands.

1 roll puff (flaky) pastry

----

1 tablespoon (15 g/½ oz) butter

Jam

2 coconuts

1¾ lb (800 g) cane sugar or white (caster) sugar

----

zest of 1 lime

----

pinch ground cinnamon

Génoise cake

8 eggs

----

9 oz (250 g) superfine (caster) sugar

----

9 oz (250 g) all-purpose (plain) flour, sifted

----

2 teaspoons vanilla extract

Cream

9 oz (250 g) cane sugar or white (caster) sugar

----

3 oz (80 g) all-purpose (plain) flour

----

4 eggs

----

1 cup (250 ml/8 fl oz) whole (full-cream) milk

----

1 vanilla bean (pod)

To make the jam, make two small holes in the top of the coconuts and remove the coconut juice. Set aside. Break open the coconuts and grate the flesh. Place the grated coconut in a saucepan with the cane sugar, coconut juice, lime zest, cinnamon and 2 cups (500 ml) water. Mix well and cook over low heat for 30 minutes.

To make the génoise, beat the eggs, then slowly add the sugar, beating constantly. Beat in the sifted flour, then the vanilla extract. Set aside.

To make the confectioner's cream, place the sugar, flour and eggs in large bowl. Beat vigorously until they form a smooth paste. In a saucepan, heat the milk with the vanilla bean. When hot, stir into the egg mixture, then set aside.

Preheat oven to 350°F (180°C/gas 4). Place the puff pastry in a buttered pie pan, or 6 individual tart pans, then add the coconut jam. Cover with the génoise and bake for 20 minutes. Serve with the confectioner's cream.

Mirliton Tarte Tatin with honey and sweet spices

Serves 6
Prep: 15 minutes
Cook: 5 minutes
Bake: 15 to 20 minutes

2¼ lb (1 kg) green
mirlitons* (chayotes)
----
8 tablespoons (100 g/
3½ oz) unsalted butter
----
zest of 1 lime
----
3 tablespoons (30 g)
superfine (caster) sugar
----
2 teaspoons vanilla sugar
----
pinch ground cinnamon
----
pinch ground malanga*
----
a grating fresh ginger
----
3 tablespoons honey
----
1 roll puff (flaky) pastry

Cut the mirlitons in quarters lengthwise. Peel them and remove the core. Cut each piece in half. Melt the butter in a skillet or frying pan over high heat; add the lime zest and fry the mirliton pieces for 3 minutes without letting them brown.

Preheat oven to 400°F (200°C/gas 6). Place the superfine sugar and vanilla sugar in 6 tart pans. Arrange the mirliton pieces on top, side by side. Sprinkle with the cinnamon and the malanga. Add the grated ginger and finally the honey. Place the pastry on top. Trim, then pinch around the edges to close. Prick with a fork to aerate during baking.

Bake for 15 minutes, then reduce the oven temperature to 300°F (150°C/gas 2) and continue baking until the pastry is golden. Remove from the oven and turn out immediately onto flat serving plates.

Tarragon granita

Serves 4
Prep: 5 minutes
Stand: 30 minutes
Freeze: 3 to 12 hours

½ cup (120 g/4 oz)
superfine (caster) sugar
----
10 sprigs tarragon and
2 teaspoons (10 g) chopped
tarragon
----
juice of 1 lime
----
scant ½ cup (100 ml/
3½ fl oz) 50-proof white
agricultural rum*

Place the tarragon sprigs, lime juice and rum in
a bowl. In a saucepan, add the sugar to 2 cups
(500 ml/18 fl oz) water and boil for 5 minutes.
Pour this syrup into the bowl. Cover with a clean
cloth and let stand to infuse for 30 minutes.

Strain the cooled mixture then pour into a freezer-
safe container. Freeze for about 3 hours. Each hour
after that, scrape with a fork until the granita
is consistent in texture. Serve in small glasses.

Tarragon granita is the quintessential
West Indian aperitif.

Honey

Banana Tarte Tatin with chocolate chips

Serves 4
Prep: 8 to 10 minutes
Cook: 10 minutes
Bake: 20 minutes

⅓ cup (90 g/3 oz) butter

----

2 oz (50 g) vanilla sugar

----

8 black-spotted bananas,
peeled and cut into thirds

----

scant 1 cup (200 g/7 oz)
semi-sweet (plain)
chocolate chips

----

1 roll puff (flaky) pastry

Melt the butter in a saucepan, add the sugar and cook until lightly caramelized. Add the bananas and brown them lightly.

Preheat oven to 350°F (180°C/gas 4). Butter a tart pan, or 4 individual tart pans, and throw in the chocolate chips. Arrange the banana pieces on top, packing them in tightly, side by side. Cover with the pastry, then trim and pinch around the edges to close. Bake for 20 minutes. As soon as you take them out of the oven, turn them out onto flat serving plates. Serve warm with banana ice cream.

Coconut sherbet

Makes 4 cups (1 litre/1¾
pints)
Prep: 15 minutes
Process: 20 to 30 minutes
Freeze: 30 minutes to 2
hours

4 coconuts

----

1 14-oz (400 g) can
sweetened condensed milk

----

pinch ground cinnamon

----

finely grated zest of
1 lime

----

1 vanilla bean (pod)

----

scant ½ cup (100 g/3½ oz)
superfine (caster) sugar

Break open the coconuts and grate the flesh. Bring
2 cups (500 ml/18 fl oz) water to a boil in a
saucepan then add the grated coconut. Cook for 5
minutes then remove from heat and set aside to
cool, then squeeze the grated coconut in a clean
cloth over a saucepan to extract the coconut milk.

Heat the coconut milk in the saucepan with the
condensed milk, cinnamon, lime zest, vanilla seeds
scraped out of the bean, and sugar. Stir well
and set aside to cool before pouring into an ice-
cream maker.

Follow the machine manufacturer's instructions to
process the sherbet. Freeze to desired firmness,
which should take between 30 minutes and 2 hours.

Passionfruit sorbet

Makes 4 cups (1 litre/
1¾ pints)
Prep: 15 minutes
Cook: 2 to 3 minutes
Process: 20 to 30 minutes
Freeze: 30 minutes to
2 hours

2¼ lb (1 kg) passionfruit
----
14 oz (400 g) superfine
(caster) sugar

½ lime

Halve each passionfruit and remove the flesh,
retaining the pulp and skins. Purée the pulp
(including the seeds) in a blender or food
processor with a small glass of water. Pass
through a sieve to remove any trace of seeds.

Bring 1 cup (250 ml/8 fl oz) water and the sugar
to a boil in a saucepan and cook for 2 to 3
minutes. Remove from heat then add the passionfruit
purée and a few drops of lime juice. Mix well
and set aside to cool before pouring into an
ice-cream maker.

Follow the machine manufacturer's instructions to
process the sorbet. Freeze to desired firmness,
which should take between 30 minutes and 2 hours.
Serve in the retained passionfruit skins.

Coconut cassava cakes

Serves 8
Stand: 48 hours
Prep: 25 minutes
Cook: 4 minutes

13 ½ lb (6 kg) cassava*
----
2 coconuts

¾ cup (180 g/6½ oz) cane
sugar or white (caster)
sugar
----
pinch ground cinnamon
----
pinch ground nutmeg
----
2 tablespoons powdered
(icing) sugar, for
sprinkling

Two days before serving, peel the cassava, wash
well, then grate finely. Place the grated flesh
in a clean cloth and squeeze over a large bowl to
extract the liquid. Let stand for 24 hours.

The next day, there should be a white paste at the
bottom of the bowl with a watery liquid above. Pour
off the water, retaining only the white paste,
which we call 'moussache' (tapioca flour). Let the
moussache stand in the sun for 24 hours to dry.
When it is dry with still a hint of moisture, sift
it like flour.

Break open the coconuts and grate the flesh,
reserving a little for sprinkling. Mix the flesh
with the sugar, then add the cinnamon, nutmeg and
moussache. Form the paste into little flat cakes.
Heat a skillet or frying pan on the stove; add the
flat cakes and cook for 2 minutes on each side.
Serve hot or cold, sprinkled with reserved grated
coconut and the powdered sugar.

Coconut bonbons

Serves 10
Prep: 3 minutes
Cook: 3 minutes

3 coconuts
----
9 oz (250 g) superfine
(caster) sugar
----
1 tablespoon grenadine
----
4 cups (1 litre/1¾ pints)
sunflower oil, for
deep-frying

Break open the coconuts and grate the flesh.
Place in a large bowl with the sugar and the
grenadine. Mix well and form the coconut paste
into small balls.

Heat the oil in a large saucepan. When very hot,
throw in the coconut balls and cook over medium
heat for 3 minutes. Drain on paper towels and allow
to cool before serving.

These sweet treats come from Reunion Island.

Coconut sweets with pink and green crowns

Serves 4
Prep: 20 minutes
Cook: 30 minutes

3 coconuts

----

scant ½ cup (100 g/3½ oz)
superfine (caster) sugar

----

zest of 1 lemon

----

grenadine

----

mint liqueur (such as
crème de menthe)

Break open the coconuts and grate the flesh. Place the sugar, grated coconut, lemon zest and 3 cups (750 ml/1½ fl oz) water in a saucepan. Cook for 30 minutes, until the water has completely evaporated.

Remove from heat then, using a wooden spoon, form into 8 little coconut cakes on a sheet of aluminum foil or baking paper, reserving about 2 tablespoons of the mixture.

In a saucepan, mix half of the reserved coconut paste with a little grenadine. Place a small ball of the grenadine coconut on 4 of the prepared cakes. Repeat the procedure with the remaining coconut and a little mint liqueur, placing little balls of the mixture on top of the remaining 4 coconut cakes.

Creole barley sugar

Serves 4
Prep: 5 minutes
Cook: 10 minutes
Stand: 10 minutes

9 oz (250 g) cane sugar or
white (caster) sugar

Place the sugar in a saucepan and cover with
a little water. Bring to a boil over low heat,
stirring constantly until the sugar has dissolved
completely. Increase the heat so that the mixture
starts to boil more rapidly, and keep boiling until
the mixture forms a consistent syrup. Remove from
the heat and set aside for 10 minutes to cool.

Pour the syrup onto an oiled marble work surface.
When the sugar is cold, cut into small discs or
ovals using a pair of scissors. Insert a small
stick into one end to make a barley-sugar lollipop.

Kilibibi

Serves 4
Prep: 20 minutes
Cook: 10 minutes

2⅓ cups (600 g/1 lb 5 oz)
popping corn
----
11 oz (300 g) cane sugar or
white (granulated) sugar
----
1 teaspoon ground cinnamon

½ teaspoon ground nutmeg

Heat a cast-iron casserole on the stove. When very
hot, pour in the popping corn. Cover and cook,
shaking the pan constantly. Keep shaking until all
the kernels have popped, then remove from heat and
set aside.

Put the sugar in a blender or food processor and
process for about a second. Remove from blender
or food processor and set aside.

Put the popcorn in the blender or food processor
and reduce to a floury consistency. Place the
sugar, cinnamon and nutmeg in a bowl. Mix well
then add the popcorn, stirring constantly. Mix
again then serve in paper cones.

The recipe for this traditional crushed-popcorn confectionery, originally from Marie Galante Island, comes straight from my childhood memories.

Lotchio

Serves 4
Prep: 15 minutes
Cook: 15 to 20 minutes

2 coconuts

----

4 cups (1 litre/1¾ pints)
sirop de batterie*

½ teaspoon ground cinnamon

----

pinch ground nutmeg

Break open the coconuts and finely grate the flesh.
Place the sirop de batterie in a saucepan then mix
in the grated coconut and the spices. Cook over
low heat for 15 to 20 minutes. When the mixture
is very thick, remove from heat. Immediately form
into little heaps on an oiled plate then set aside
to cool.

Coconut bars

Serves 6
Prep: 40 minutes
Cook: 10 to 15 minutes

1 coconut
----
pinch ground cinnamon
----
scant 1 cup (200 g/7 oz)
cane sugar or white
(caster) sugar
----
grated zest of 1 lemon
----
1 teaspoon vanilla extract
----
1 teaspoon almond extract

Make two small holes in the top of the coconut and remove the coconut juice; set aside. Break open the coconut and grate enough of the flesh in long strips to measure 14 oz (400 g).

Place the grated coconut, cinnamon, sugar, lemon zest, vanilla and almond extracts in a saucepan. Mix well. Cook over low heat for 10 to 15 minutes, slowly adding 1 cup (250 ml/8 fl oz) of the coconut juice. Stir constantly until the mixture caramelizes.

Remove from heat then put small heaps of the mixture on an oiled plate. Form into bars, then set aside to cool.

Doucelette

Serves 10
Prep: 40 minutes
Cook: 50 minutes
Stand: 30 minutes

3 coconuts
----
scant 1 cup (200 ml/7 fl
oz) whole (full-cream)
milk
----
1 vanilla bean (pod)

2¼ lb (1 kg) cane sugar or
white (caster) sugar
----
1 14-oz (400 g) can
sweetened condensed milk
----
pinch ground cinnamon
----
grated zest of 1 lime

Break open the coconuts and finely grate the flesh. Pour the whole milk over the grated coconut then squeeze in a clean cloth over a bowl to extract the liquid. Split the vanilla bean lengthwise then scrape out the black seeds using the tip of a knife.

Heat the sugar in a heavy-based saucepan. When it caramelizes, add the coconut milk, condensed milk, cinnamon, vanilla seeds and lime zest, then cook over medium heat for 50 minutes, stirring constantly with a wooden spoon.

Pour the mixture onto an oiled cookie sheet or baking tray and set aside for 30 minutes to cool. Cut the coconut mixture into small squares and chill in the refrigerator or freezer before turning them out.

Banana jam

Makes 6 small jars
Prep: 15 minutes
Cook: 15 minutes

8 very ripe, black-spotted
bananas
----
scant 1 cup (200 g/7 oz)
superfine (caster) sugar
----
juice of 1 orange
----
juice of 1 lime
----
1 vanilla bean (pod)

Place the peeled bananas in a bowl and mash using a fork. Add the sugar and the orange and lime juices. Mix well to form a smooth purée. Place this mixture in a saucepan and cook over low heat, stirring constantly.

Split the vanilla bean and add to the saucepan. Continue cooking for 10 to 15 minutes, until the banana browns. Set aside to cool, then refrigerate.

Fill 6 small jars with airtight lids with the jam. Seal tightly then cool by placing in a bowl of cold water. Once cooled, store jars in the refrigerator or in a cool cupboard; refrigerate after opening.

Barbadine jam

Makes 6 small jars
Prep: 10 minutes
Cook: 25 minutes

3½ cups (700 g/1 lb 8½ oz)
superfine (caster) sugar
----
juice of 1 lime

2¼ lb (1 kg) barbadine*
(giant granadilla) flesh,
thinly sliced

In a saucepan, heat the sugar with 1 cup (250 ml/ 8 fl oz) water and lime juice and bring to a boil. Add the barbadine flesh and cook for 25 minutes.

Fill 6 small jars with airtight lids with the jam. Seal tightly then cool by placing in a bowl of cold water. Once cooled, store jars in the refrigerator or in a cool cupboard; refrigerate after opening.

Coconut jam

Makes 6 small jars
Prep: 40 minutes
Cook: 25 minutes

2 coconuts
----
11 oz (300 g) superfine
(caster) sugar
----
1 cinnamon stick
----
grated zest of 1 lime

Break open the coconuts and grate the flesh.

Pour 1 cup (250 ml/8 fl oz) water into a saucepan, add the sugar and the cinnamon stick and bring to a boil. When the sugar has completely dissolved, add the grated coconut and the lime zest, then cook over low heat, stirring constantly, for 20 to 25 minutes, until the coconut flesh becomes transparent.

Fill 6 small jars with airtight lids with the jam. Seal tightly then cool by placing in a bowl of cold water. Once cooled, store jars in the refrigerator or in a cool cupboard; refrigerate after opening.

Cane sugar

Julie mango jam

Makes 6 small jars
Prep: 10 minutes
Cook: 35 minutes

4 large Julie mangoes*,
peeled and finely sliced

3½ cups (700 g/1 lb 8½ oz)
superfine (caster) sugar

----

juice of ½ lime

----

1 vanilla bean (pod)

Wash and peel the mangoes then finely slice the flesh. Place the sugar, 7 fl oz (200 ml) water and the lime juice in a saucepan. Cook for 5 minutes then add the mango. Add the split vanilla bean and cook over medium heat for 30 minutes more.

Remove the vanilla bean and skim any foam off the mixture if necessary. Fill 6 small jars with airtight lids with the jam. Seal tightly then cool by placing in a bowl of cold water. Once cooled, store jars in the refrigerator or in a cool cupboard; refrigerate after opening.

Papaya jam

Makes 6 small jars
Prep: 10 minutes
Cook: 1 hour

1 large, ripe papaya
(2¼ lb/1 kg)

1¾ lb (800 g) superfine
(caster) sugar

----

juice of 1 lime

----

1 vanilla bean (pod)

Peel the papaya. Using a teaspoon, carefully remove the black seeds, then chop the flesh into large dice. Place the sugar, 1 cup (250 ml/8 fl oz) water, and lime juice in a saucepan. Bring to a boil, then cook for 30 minutes. Add the papaya and the vanilla bean, then cook for 30 minutes more.

Remove the vanilla bean. Fill 6 small jars with airtight lids with the jam. Seal tightly then cool by placing in a bowl of cold water. Once cooled, store jars in the refrigerator or in a cool cupboard; refrigerate after opening.

Sweet potato jam

Makes 6 small jars
Prep: 10 minutes
Cook: 1 hour 10 minutes

1¾ lb (800 g) sweet
potatoes

----

scant 1 cup (200 g/7 oz)
superfine (caster) sugar

----

1 vanilla bean (pod)

----

1 cinnamon stick

----

2 fresh mint leaves,
chopped

Peel the sweet potatoes and cut into large dice. Blanch them in boiling water for 15 minutes, then drain. Place the sugar, 2 cups (500 ml/18 fl oz) water, vanilla bean, cinnamon stick and mint leaves in a saucepan. Cook for 10 to 15 minutes to make a syrup. Add the sweet potatoes, then simmer over very low heat for about 40 minutes.

Fill 6 small jars with airtight lids with the jam. Seal tightly then cool by placing in a bowl of cold water. Once cooled, store jars in the refrigerator or in a cool cupboard; refrigerate after opening.

Guava jelly

Makes 6 to 8 small jars
Prep: 15 minutes
Cook: 1 hour

2¼ lb (1 kg) guavas

3½ cups (700 g/1 lb 8½ oz)
superfine (caster) sugar

----

1 vanilla bean (pod)

----

pinch of freshly grated
nutmeg

----

2 pinches ground cinnamon

Peel the guavas and chop into small pieces,
retaining the peelings. Place the guava pieces and
the peelings in a large saucepan. Add enough water
to cover, bring to a boil and cook for 20 minutes.

Strain the stewed fruit, discarding the solids,
then add the sugar, vanilla bean, nutmeg and
cinnamon to the liquid. Return to the saucepan
and cook, stirring constantly, for 40 minutes.
Check whether the jelly is cooked by pouring a few
drops onto a plate: if they set quickly, the jelly
is ready.

Fill 6 to 8 small jars with airtight lids with
the jam. Seal tightly then cool by placing in a
bowl of cold water. Once cooled, store jars in
the refrigerator or a cool cupboard; refrigerate
after opening.

Roselle jelly

Makes 8 small jars
Prep: 40 minutes
Cook: 50 minutes

2¼ lb (1 kg) roselle
(hibiscus) flowers

3¾ cups (750 g/1 lb 10 oz)
superfine (caster) sugar

----

juice of 2 limes

Remove the calyces from the flowers and discard.
Place the petals in a bowl of water. Rinse well.

Place the sugar and the lime juice in a saucepan
with ½ pint (300 ml) water. Cook for 10 minutes,
then add the flower petals and cook for 40 minutes
more. Skim the surface from time to time to remove
any foam. When cooked, pass the whole mixture
through a strainer.

Fill 8 small jars with airtight lids with the
jam. Seal tightly then cool by placing them in a
bowl of cold water. Once cooled, store jars in
the refrigerator or a cool cupboard; refrigerate
after opening.

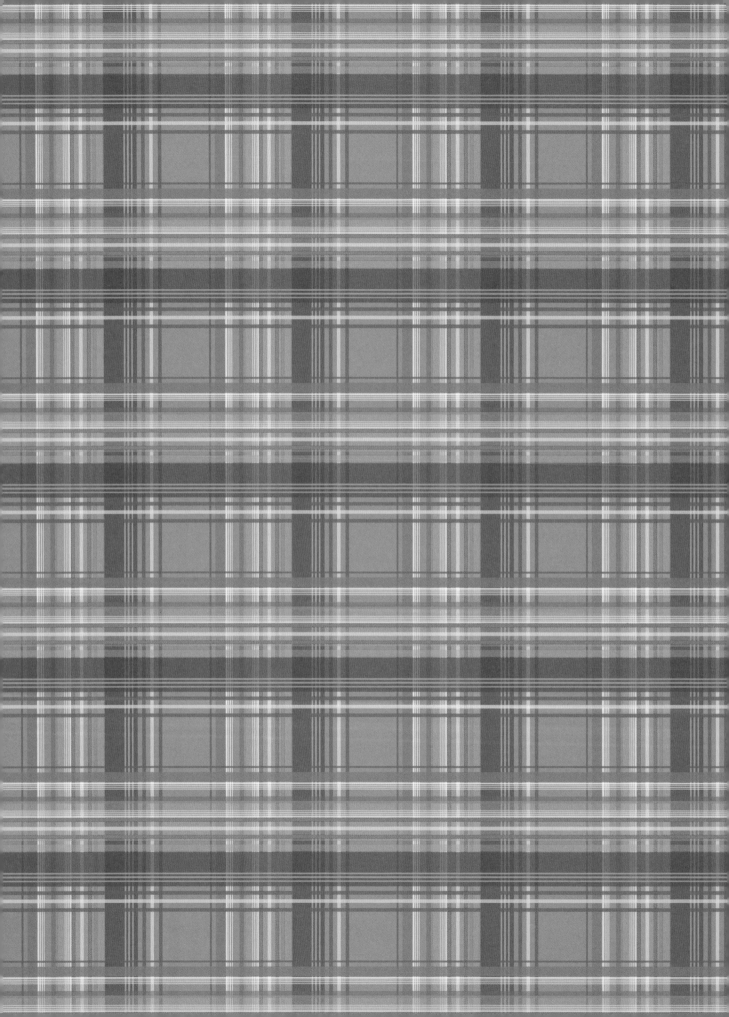

Ti'punch

and

company

Rum

St Louis

ILE
de
MARIE GALANTE

Père Labat
Grand Bourg

A la fin du 17ème siècle, le Père Labat
distillation du "Vezou" fermenté par
cannes fraîches récoltées locale
Marie Galante, des anci
assurait au nouveau pro
incomparable et une noto
ce jour.

Babette's punch

Serves 1
Prep: 8 to 10 minutes

¼ cup (50 ml/2 fl oz)
white rum

¼ cup (50 ml/2 fl oz)
triple sec

¼ cup (50 ml/2 fl oz)
mandarin liqueur
----
1 tablespoon mandarin syrup
----
crushed ice

¼ orange, cut into small
pieces

¼ lime, cut into small
pieces
----
1 tablespoon grenadine

Pour the rum, triple sec, mandarin liqueur and
mandarin syrup into a large cocktail glass and
mix well. Add the crushed ice, then the pieces
of orange and lime, squeezing them before dropping
them in.

Gently add the grenadine so that it stays at the
bottom of the glass. Serve immediately.

Traditional Guadeloupean ti'punch

Serves 1
Prep: 5 minutes

¼ lime, cut into small
pieces
----
2 tablespoons cane sugar
or white (caster) sugar
----
scant ¼ cup (40 ml/
1½ fl oz) 50 proof white
agricultural rum*

Place the lime pieces in a punch glass then add the
cane sugar. Using a teaspoon, crush the lime pieces
to extract their juice and mix it with the sugar.
Add the rum and mix well. The punch is ready.

In Martinique this punch is served with ice cubes.

Ti'punch is served in small glasses
called 'punch glasses' We call it
'ti'punch' because the glass is small
(petit) which means you can drink
several!

Coconut punch

Serves 1
Prep: 40 minutes
Chill: 24 hours

1 coconut

----

scant ⅓ cup (60 ml/
3 fl oz) white rum

----

1 tablespoon coconut syrup
or cane (sugar) syrup

----

pinch ground cinnamon

----

pinch ground nutmeg

----

1 vanilla bean (pod)

Break open the coconut and finely grate the flesh. Place the grated coconut in a bowl with ⅔ cup (150 ml/¼ pint) boiling water and set aside to infuse. When the mixture is cooled, extract the milk into a bowl by squeezing the flesh in a clean cloth.

Pour the coconut milk into a glass then add the rum, coconut syrup, cinnamon and nutmeg. Split the vanilla bean and scrape out the small black seeds with the tip of a knife. Add the vanilla seeds to the mixture. Chill for 24 hours and serve over crushed ice.

Passion punch

Serves 2
Prep: 10 minutes

11 oz (300 g) passionfruit

----

scant ½ cup (100 g/3 ½ oz)
superfine (caster) sugar

----

1 cup (250 ml/8 fl oz)
white rum

Halve the passionfruit; remove the pulp and seeds and place them in a blender with the sugar and ⅓ cup (100 ml/3½ fl oz) water. Purée for 2 to 3 minutes, then pass through a fine-mesh sieve 3 to 4 times to remove all trace of the crushed seeds. Add the white rum and mix well.

Pour into a bottle, seal with an airtight lid, and refrigerate. Serve cold over crushed ice.

Punch d'amour

Serves 4
Prep: 15 minutes
Steep: 2 months

3½ oz (100 g) bois bandé*,
grated

----

scant ½ cup (100 g/3½ oz)
grated fresh ginger

----

2 vanilla beans (pods),
split lengthwise and
coarsely chopped

----

4 tablespoons clear honey

----

pinch ground cinnamon

----

2 cups (500 ml/18 fl oz)
white rum

Place the bois bandé, ginger, vanilla, honey, cinnamon and rum in a canning or preserving jar and seal tightly. Leave the jar in a cupboard for 2 months to steep. Serve straight in small glasses.

Steeped mombin punch

Makes 4 cups
(1 litre/1¾ pints)
Prep: 10 minutes
Steep: 2 months

1 lb 2 oz (500 g) mombin*,
washed and scored

----

4 cups (1 litre/1¾ pints)
50-proof white
agricultural rum*

⅔ cup (150 g/5 oz) cane
sugar or white sugar

Place the mombins in a canning or preserving jar
with the sugar and rum; seal tightly. Let stand in
the sun for 8 days, then leave the jar in a
cupboard for 2 months to steep.

Serve steeped punches in conical tasting glasses, to conserve their aromas.

Steeped guava punch

Makes 4 cups (1 litre/
1¾ pints)
Prep: 10 minutes
Steep: 2 months

1 lb 2 oz (500 g) very
ripe guava, washed and
quartered

----

4 cups (1 litre/1¾ pints)
white rum

⅔ cup (150 g) superfine
(caster) sugar

Place the guavas in a canning or preserving jar
with the sugar and rum; seal tightly. Let stand in
the sun for 8 days, then leave the jar in a
cupboard for 2 months to steep. Strain the punch
just before drinking.

Steeped ginger punch

Makes 4 cups (1 litre/
1¾ pints)
Prep: 10 minutes
Steep: 2 months

scant 1 cup (200 g/7 oz)
grated unpeeled
fresh ginger

----

scant 1 cup (200 g/7 oz)
superfine (caster) sugar

----

4 cups (1 litre/1¾ pints)
50-proof white agricultural
rum*

Place the grated ginger in a canning or preserving
jar with the sugar and rum; seal tightly. Let stand
in the sun for 8 days, then leave the jar in a
cupboard for 2 months to steep.

Just before drinking, strain the punch to remove
the ginger pulp. Serve over crushed ice.

Serves 4
Prep: 20 minutes
Steep: 1 month

14 oz (400 g) ambarellas*,
washed and scored

⅔ cup (150 g/5 oz)
superfine (caster) sugar
----
6 cups (1.5 litres/
2½ pints) 50-proof white
agricultural rum*

Steeped ambarella punch

Place the ambarellas in a saucepan with the sugar and ¾ cup (200 ml/7 fl oz) water. Bring to a boil and cook for 10 minutes. Remove from heat and set aside to cool.

Pour into a canning or preserving jar and add the white rum. Leave the jar in a cupboard for 1 month to steep. Strain and serve over crushed ice.

Serves 4
Prep: 10 minutes
Steep: 3½ months

1 lb 2 oz (500 g)
vegetarian chiles*
(chillis), halved
lengthwise (if
unavailable, substitute
whole serrano chile)
----
4 cups (1 litre/1¾ pints)
50-proof white
agricultural rum*

¾ cup (200 g/7 oz)
superfine (caster) sugar

Steeped vegetarian chile punch

Place the chiles in a canning or preserving jar with the sugar and the rum; seal tightly. Let stand in the sun for 10 days, then leave the jar in a cupboard for 3 months to steep. Strain and serve cold. (If using serrano chiles, do not cut them in half - instead prick the skin with a fork.)

Serves 4
Prep: 16 minutes
Steep: 1 month

1 lb 2 oz (500 g)
tamarind*, washed and
scored

¾ cup (200 g/7 oz)
superfine (caster) sugar
----
4 cups (1 litre/1¾ pints)
white rum

Steeped tamarind punch

Place the tamarind in a saucepan with the sugar and ¾ cup (200 ml/7 fl oz) water. Bring to a boil and cook for 10 minutes. Remove from heat and set aside to cool.

Pour into a canning or preserving jar and add the white rum. Leave the jar in a cupboard to steep for 1 month. Strain and serve over crushed ice.

Babette's pina colada

Serves 1
Prep: 20 minutes

1 Victoria pineapple*,
peeled and chopped

1¼ oz (30 ml/1 fl oz)
coconut milk

1½ oz (40 ml/2 fl oz)
white rum
----
1 tablespoon superfine
(caster) sugar
----
2 pinches ground cinnamon

½ tablespoon pure vanilla
extract
----
crushed ice

Purée the pineapple in a blender. Place the pulp
in a clean cloth and squeeze over a bowl to extract
the juice.

Pour the pineapple juice, coconut milk, rum, sugar,
1 pinch of the ground cinnamon, the vanilla and the
crushed ice in a blender. Purée the mixture then
pour into a glass. Sprinkle with the remaining
cinnamon and serve cold.

Mulled wine

Serves 6
Prep: 15 minutes

2 cups (500 ml/18 fl oz)
Bordeaux or other full-
bodied red wine
----
1 cinnamon stick
----
2 whole cloves
----
a grating fresh ginger
----
grated zest of 1 lime
----
1 orange, sliced

¼ cup (50 g/2 fl oz)
superfine (caster) sugar

⅓ cup (100 ml/4 fl oz)
white rum

Mix the wine, cinnamon stick, cloves, ginger, lime zest, orange and sugar in a saucepan. Bring to a boil and cook over low heat for 5 to 6 minutes, then pass through a sieve. Add the rum just before serving; serve hot in a cocktail glass.

West Indian caress

Serves 6
Prep: 10 minutes

1 cup (250 ml/8 fl oz)
banana juice
----
1 cup (250 ml/8 fl oz)
passionfruit juice
----
1 cup (250 ml/8 fl oz)
guava juice
----
1 cup (250 ml/8 fl oz)
pineapple juice
----
3 tablespoons sirop
d' orgeat (almond syrup)
----
3 tablespoons grenadine
----
1 lime, zested

Mix the fruit juices with the sirop d' orgeat (almond syrup) and the grenadine in a bowl. Add the lime zest and serve cold.

Caribbean Planter's punch

Serves 10
Prep: 15 minutes

1 cup (250 ml/8 fl oz)
guava juice
----

1 cup (250 ml/8 fl oz)
banana juice
----

1 cup (250 ml/8 fl oz)
grapefruit juice
----

1 cup (250 ml/8 fl oz)
passionfruit juice
----

1 cup (250 ml/8 fl oz)
pineapple juice
----

1 cup (250 ml/8 fl oz)
orange juice
----

2 cups (500 ml/18 fl oz)
aged rum (rhum vieux)
----

3 tablespoons grenadine
----

4 tablespoons cane (sugar)
syrup
----

pinch ground cinnamon
----

1 tablespoon angostura
bitters*
----

3 passionfruit
----

1 orange, sliced
----

1 lime, sliced

Pour all the fruit juices into a bowl. Add the
rum, grenadine, cane syrup, cinnamon and bitters.
Mix well.

Halve the passionfruit; remove the pulp and seeds
and add them to the juice mixture. Add the orange
and lime slices. Refrigerate until cool then serve
over ice cubes.

Madiana

Serves 4
Prep: 5 minutes

4 juicy oranges
----

4 grapefruit
----

2 limes
----

3 tablespoons superfine
(caster) sugar
----

a few fresh mint leaves
----

a few pieces of citrus
peel

Squeeze the juice from the citrus fruits into
a bowl, then add the sugar and 2 cups (500 ml/
18 fl oz) water. Mix the Madiana well and serve
cold, garnished with a few chopped mint leaves
and a twist of citrus peel.

Pineapple frappé

Serves 4
Prep: 5 minutes

2 large, very ripe
pineapples, peeled and
diced
----
4 cups (1 litre/1¾ pints)
whole (full-cream) milk
----
3 oz (80 g) superfine
(caster) sugar
----
5 ice cubes, crushed
----
1 tablespoon grenadine

Place the pineapple, milk, sugar and crushed ice in
a blender. Blend for 1 minute, then pass through a
sieve. Serve cold. Add the grenadine as decoration.

Banana frappé

Serves 4
Prep: 20 minutes

3 medium bananas (350 g/
12 oz), cut into pieces
----
4 cups (1 litre/1¾ pints)
whole (full-cream) milk

½ tablespoon grated
lemon zest
----
4 tablespoons superfine
(caster) sugar

½ tablespoon vanilla
extract
----
5 ice cubes, crushed

Place the bananas, milk, lemon zest, sugar and
vanilla in a blender. Add the ice cubes and blend
at high speed for 1 minute. Pour into glasses and
serve cold.

Passionfruit frappé

Serves 4
Prep: 10 minutes

14 oz (400 g) passionfruit
----
1 tablespoon grated
lemon zest

⅓ cup (80 g/3 oz)
superfine (caster) sugar,
plus additional to taste
----
4 cups (1 litre/1¾ pints)
whole (full-cream) milk
----
5 ice cubes, crushed

Halve the passionfruit; remove the pulp and seeds and place them in a blender with the lemon zest, sugar and milk. Blend for 1 to 2 minutes then pass through a sieve 2 to 3 times until there is no trace of crushed seeds. Add the ice cubes then blend once more. Add sugar to taste, if desired. Serve immediately.

Papaya frappé

Serves 4
Prep: 10 minutes

14 oz (400 g) very ripe
papaya
----
4 cups (1 litre/1¾ pints)
whole (full-cream) milk

⅓ cup (80 g/3 oz)
superfine (caster) sugar
----
1 tablespoon grated
lime zest
----
2 tablespoons lemon juice

½ vanilla bean (pod)
----
5 ice cubes, crushed

Peel the papayas and remove the black seeds using a teaspoon. Cut the flesh into large dice. Place the milk, sugar, lime zest and juice, vanilla, papaya and ice cubes in a blender. Blend for 1 minute then strain. Serve immediately, very cold.

Schrub

Makes 4 cups (1 litre/
1¾ pints)
Prep: 5 minutes
Steep: 2 months

4 oranges, ideally organic
West Indian oranges
----
4 cups (1 litre/1¾ pints)
white rum

¾ cup (200 g/7 oz)
superfine (caster) sugar

Peel the oranges, retaining the peel. Leave the peel in the sun to dry for 1 week. When very dry, break up into little pieces and place in a canning or preserving jar.

Make a light syrup by boiling the sugar and ⅔ cup (150 ml/¼ pint) water for about 5 minutes. Pour the syrup into the jar. Add the rum, seal tightly, and leave in the sun for 10 days, then at room temperature for 1 month. Serve in small glasses without ice.

Pineapple nectar

Serves 6
Prep: 10 minutes

2 large, very ripe
pineapples, peeled and
diced

⅓ cup (80 g/3 oz)
superfine (caster) sugar

Place pineapple in a blender with the sugar and
4 cups (1 litre/1¾ pints) water; blend then strain.
Serve cold.

Passionfruit nectar

Serves 6
Prep: 10 minutes

14 oz (400 g) passionfruit

⅓ cup (80 g/3 oz)
superfine (caster) sugar

Halve each passionfruit; remove the pulp and place
it in a blender with the sugar and 1 cup (250 ml/
8 fl oz) water; blend for 2 to 3 minutes.

Pass through a sieve 2 to 3 times, until there is
no trace of crushed seed. Refrigerate. Add more
sugar to taste. Serve cold.

Ginger nectar

Serves 4
Prep: 20 minutes

⅔ cup (150 g/5 oz) grated
fresh ginger

⅓ cup (80 g) superfine
(caster) sugar

Place ginger and sugar in a blender with ¾ cup
(200 ml/7 fl oz) water. Purée for 2 to 3 minutes.

Pour 4 cups (1 litre/1¾ pints) of boiling water
over the ginger purée. Cover with a clean cloth
and let stand to infuse until the mixture is cool.
Pass through a fine-mesh sieve and refrigerate.
Add more sugar before serving if desired.

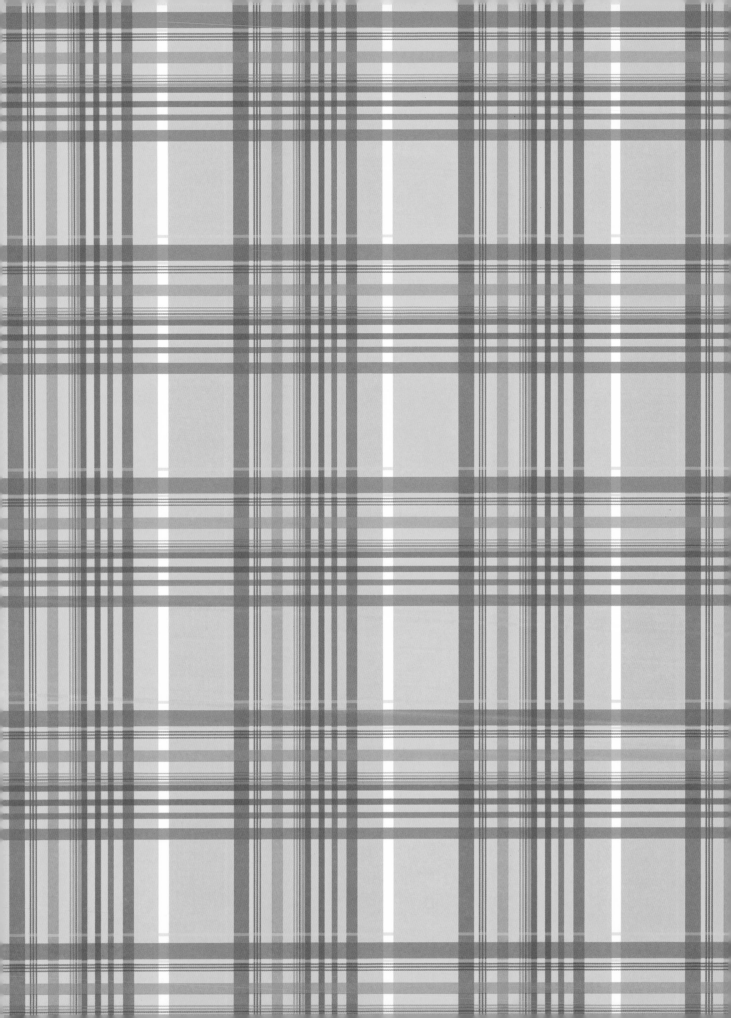

Glossary,
Suppliers
and Index

Glossary

Acras
A fritter usually enjoyed at breakfast and often made from salt cod.

Agricultural rum
West Indian artisanal white alcohol derived from sugarcane; its alcohol content is reduced to 50 and 55 proof (25 to 27½ percent alcohol) on Guadeloupe by the addition of distilled or spring water.

Ambarella (golden apple)
Ovoid fruit, yellow-orange when ripe, used notably in jams; more recently used for the juice of the still-green fruit.

Angostura bitters
A liquid flavoring made from herbs and spices that is used in planter's punch instead of cinnamon.

Arôme Patrelle
A natural glucose-based food coloring available in specialty markets and online.

Bain Marie
A water bath that allows delicate dishes to cook gently. Place the container of food to be cooked in a larger, shallow pan. Add hot water to surround the dish of food to a height of about 1 in (2.5 cm) and cook. A bain Marie is often called a double boiler.

Barbadine (giant granadilla)
Fruit whose roots are considered to be potent narcotics but whose sweet and sour pulp can be eaten without risk.

Bélangère
West Indian eggplant (aubergine) with white-streaked purple skin.

Bird's eye chile
Red or green, small, hot chili pepper also known as 'piri-piri,' 'peri-peri,' 'pili-pili,' and the 'angry chile.'

Blaff
A style of cooking fish or shellfish in water and spices. Its name comes from the sound made when you put the fish in the spicy court bouillon (stock).

Bois bande
Bark of Richeria grandis, also called 'bois d'homme' (man wood), renowned for its alleged effect on virility.

Bois d'inde
Condiment found either as leaves or as dried seeds, used like bay leaves in marinades or seasonings.

Bouquet garni
Bunches of various combinations of herbs added during cooking and removed before serving. A classic bouquet garni is 3 sprigs fresh parsley, 1 sprig fresh thyme and 1 bay leaf. Herbs are tied together or, when dried herbs are used, combined in small muslin bags.

Camaron
Large prawn with a tough shell and a strong taste.

Cassava
Also called manioc and yucca, a root 2 to 3 inches in diameter and typically 6 to 12 inches long; available year-round in Latin American and Caribbean markets.

Chadron

Indigenous sea urchins, as they are called in the French West Indies.

Chatrou

Octopus of the French West Indies.

Chayote

Vegetable with yellow or green skin, slightly prickly to the touch; known in North America as 'mirliton.'

Cockles

Small shellfish, related to the clam, with pale and delicate flesh. Shells are normally white or cream and roughly circular in shape with ribs radiating from the shell's hinge.

Colombo

Spice mix that includes garlic, red chile, turmeric, cilantro (coriander) and mustard seeds.

Conch

Gastropod mollusc with firm white flesh. Imported conch is available vacuum packed or dried but it is illegal to harvest conch in the USA. If unavailable, substitute whelks, although the flavor will differ.

Crème fraîche

Thick and smooth soured cream. Crème fraîche found in specialty stores in North America is expensive. For a recipe to make it at home, see page 62.

Giraumon

An indigenous pumpkin of the French West Indies. If unavailable, substitute other varieties of pumpkin, although the flavor will differ.

Graines à roussir

Mixture of fenugreek, cumin and yellow mustard seeds.

Julie mango

Oval, flattened, pale green and red mango with non-fibrous flesh. If unavailable, subsitute very ripe mangoes of other varieties.

Lardons

Small pieces of thick-cut bacon, sold ready-chopped. If unavailable, substitute thick rashers of bacon cut lengthwise into strips and then into small dice.

Madère

Tuber whose hearty leaves and stalks are also eaten; called 'dachine' in Martinique and 'madère' in Guadeloupe.

Malanga

Versatile tuber (technically a corm, a compressed underground stem) that resembles sweet potato and, like potatoes, contains lots of starch.

Masala

Roasted and ground spice mix, often including cinnamon, cumin, nutmeg and cardamom.

Matatou

Land crab fricassee.

Mirliton

See Chayote.

Mombin

Fragrant small fruit, similar to plum.

Ouassou
Large crayfish from Guadeloupe.

Pac
Small wild pig from Guyana.

Pigeon peas
Small, round peas, available dried, split, fresh, frozen, or canned. If unavailable, substitute with yellow- or black-eyed peas.

Plantain
A close relative of the banana, this greenish to yellow or black boat-shaped fruit can be eaten raw when extremely ripe (black). However, it is mostly used in cooked dishes.

Quatre épices
A finely ground 'four spice' mixture often including white pepper, nutmeg, ginger, cinnamon, or cloves.

Red paste (beurre rouge)
Condiment made from achiote, the fruit of the lipstick tree; seeds are taken from the fruit then crushed in oil, when they turn red.

Scotch bonnet chile
Small, extremely hot lantern-shape chile; it comes in a range of colors, from light green to red.

Sirop de batterie
Syrup made from cooked, concentrated sugar cane juice; available in specialty markets and online.

Sousaki
This term refers to when an ingredient is soaked in salt, garlic and lime.

Tamarind
Fruit often sold pressed into compact blocks; it is used as a condiment.

Ti'figue
Very green cooking banana or plantain.

Tripe
Meat prepared from the stomach of various animals. Before cooking, trim if necessary. Wash thoroughly, soaking overnight, and blanch for 30 minutes in salted water. Wash well again, drain and cut for cooking.

Vegetarian chile
Small, mild chile; if unavailable, substitute rocotillo chile or cayenne pepper. For punch, substitute serrano chile.

Yam
Tuber with brown, tough, inedible, bark-like skin and white, yellow or even purple flesh.

Z'habitant
Large indigenous freshwater prawns of French West Indies resembling large Mediterranean prawns, with which they can be substituted if necessary.

Suppliers

Many of the ingredients listed in this book are available from specialty stores or from Caribbean food suppliers online. Here are some online sources of Caribbean ingredients. These are frequently available fresh, frozen, canned, dried or vacuum packed.

www.walkerswood.com

www.afrocaribbeanfoods.com

www.sams247.com

www.buygracefoods.com

We have also listed possible alternative ingredients where suitable. These can be found within the recipes themselves and also in the glossary on page 354.

Note

All spoon measurements are level. 1 teaspoon = 5 ml; 1 tablespoon = 15 ml. Australian standard tablespoons are 20 ml, so Australian readers are advised to use 3 teaspoons in place of 1 tablespoon when measuring small quantities of flour, cornflour, etc. All cup and spoon measurements are level. 1 cup = 8 fluid ounces; 1 teaspoon = 5 ml; 1 tablespoon = 15 ml. Both metric and imperial measures are used in this book. Follow one set of measurements throughout, not a mixture, as they are not interchangeable.

Unless otherwise stated, eggs are assumed to be large and individual vegetables and fruits, such as onions and apples, are assumed to be medium.

Cooking times are for guidance only, as individual ovens vary. If using a fan oven, follow the manufacturer's instructions concerning oven temperatures.

If recipes include raw or very lightly cooked eggs, these should be avoided by the elderly, infants, pregnant women, convalescents, and anyone with an impaired immune system.

Index

Babette de Rozières

Following a period as an announcer and production
assistant for ORTF, the French broadcasting service,
Babette de Rozières launched her culinary career
in a tiny restaurant a stone's throw from the Folies
Bergères in Paris.

Her love of challenge led her, firstly to run a
restaurant in Saint Tropez and then, in 1981, to
open her own establishment in her birthplace of
Guadeloupe in the French Antilles. A few years
later, she returned to Paris, where she is head
chef and manager of La Table de Babette, an acclaimed
restaurant that is renowned for its Creole cuisine.

Phaidon Press Inc.
180 Varick Street
New York, NY 10014

Phaidon Press Limited
Regent's Wharf
All Saints Street
London N1 9PA

www.phaidon.com

First published in English 2007
Reprinted in paperback 2010
© 2007 Phaidon Press Limited

First published in French as
Festins Créoles by Marabout in 2006.
© Marabout

ISBN 978 0 7148 5684 1
A CIP catalogue record of this book
is available from the British Library.

Translated from the French by
Nicola Young
Cover and typography by Julia Hasting
Printed in China